THE FEMALE IMAGINATION AND THE MODERNIST AESTHETIC

Studies in Gender and Culture

A series edited by Wendy Martin, Queens College, City University of New York

Volume 1   THE FEMALE IMAGINATION AND THE MODERNIST AESTHETIC
edited by Sandra M. Gilbert and Susan Gubar

Additional volumes in preparation

ISSN 0889-3128

This book is part of a series. The publisher will accept continuation orders which may be cancelled at any time and which provide for automatic billing and shipping of each title in the series upon publication. Please write for details.

THE FEMALE IMAGINATION AND THE MODERNIST AESTHETIC

Edited by
SANDRA M. GILBERT
Princeton University

SUSAN GUBAR
Indiana University

Gordon and Breach Science Publishers
New York   London   Paris   Montreux   Tokyo

© 1986 by Gordon and Breach, Science Publishers, Inc.
Post Office Box 161, 1820 Montreux 2, Switzerland.
All rights reserved.

Gordon and Breach Science Publishers

Post Office Box 786
Cooper Station
New York, New York 10276
United States of America

Post Office Box 197
London WC2E 9PX
England

58, rue Lhomond
75005 Paris
France

14-9 Okubo 3-chome
Shinjuku-ku, Tokyo 160
Japan

The articles published in this book first appeared in the journal *Women's Studies*, Volume 13, Numbers 1 and 2.

Library of Congress Cataloging-in-Publication Data

The Female imagination and the modernist aesthetic.

(Studies in gender and culture, ISSN 0889-3128 ; v.1)
"The articles published in this book first appeared in the journal Women's studies, volume 13, numbers 1 and 2"—T.p. verso.
1. American literature—20th century—History and criticism. 2. Women in literature. 3. English literature—20th century—History and criticism.
4. Modernism (Literature) 5. Sex role in literature.
6. Feminism and literature. I. Gilbert, Sandra M.
II. Gubar, Susan, 1944—   . III. Series.
PS228.W65F46   1986   820'.9' 9287   86-22790
ISBN 0-677-21580-0

ISBN: 0-677-21580-0. ISSN: 0889-3128. No part of this book may be reproduced or utilized in any form or by any means, electronic or mechanical, including photocopying and recording, or by any information storage or retrieval system, without permission in writing from the publishers. Printed in Great Britain by Whitstable Litho Ltd., Whitstable, Kent.

CONTENTS

SERIES PREFACE

The Female Imagination and the Modernist Aesthetic is the first publication in the scholarly series of books and monographs, *Studies in Gender and Culture*. For almost two decades gender studies has been one of the most intellectually challenging areas of investigation in contemporary intellectual life. This series provides an ongoing forum for the presentation of scholarship and criticism about gender issues in the fields of anthropology, art, biology, economics, history, law, literature, the physical sciences, political science, and sociology.

This collection of essays edited by Sandra Gilbert and Susan Gubar addresses topics that are central to feminist scholarship and gender studies, such as the relationship of the female literary tradition to the larger literary context and the inter-connection of social and sexual identity with historic and economic events. As Gilbert and Gubar point out in the introductory essay to this volume, the modernist period marks an unusually powerful convergence of feminist and historical issues. Questions of the relationship of gender to war, masculine and feminine aesthetic priorities, and the social construction of personal and public identity figure prominently in this collection. This volume is the first in a series of inquiries into the field of gender studies — a continuing area of scholarly exploration for *Studies in Gender and Culture*.

Wendy Martin

Introduction: The female imagination and the modernist aesthetic

SANDRA M. GILBERT

Department of English, Princeton University

and

SUSAN GUBAR

Department of English, Indiana University, Bloomington

WHAT IS the relationship of the female imagination to the modernist aesthetic? Alienated, dispossessed or excluded from culture, women might seem to be the prototypical *poètes maudit* and thus the first modernists. As critics including Hélène Cixous, Margaret Homans, and Rachel Blau DuPlessis suggest, the strategies women writers devised for themselves as they confronted a patriarchal literary tradition might seem to furnish models for modernism.[1] Certainly, techniques such as subversive parody, disruption of linear plot, opening up of form, or fragmentation of point of view characterize the work of twentieth-century writers from Pound, Eliot, and Joyce to Beckett and Nabokov. Certainly, too, the paradigmatic modernist sees himself as ensnared in the same web of "silence, exile, and cunning" that has both confined and delivered women writers since the nineteenth-century. It could even be argued, then, that in their problematic relationship to the tradition of authority, as well as to the authority of tradition, women writers are the major precursors of all 20th-century modernists, the *avant garde* of the *avant garde*, so to speak.

Women's Studies, 1986
Vol. 13, pp. 1-10
0049-7878/86/1302-0001 $18.50/0

A few summers ago we directed an NEH Seminar for College Teachers which addressed just these questions. Organized into four units, our eight-week project focused on feminism, modernism, and feminist criticism. Specifically, we examined, first, "*Fin de Siècle* Fantasies"; second, "the Great War and the Battle of the Sexes"; third, "Transformations of Sexuality"; and fourth, "Revisions of Religion." Throughout we attempted to set major works by male modernists against major works by their female contemporaries. For example, we compared turn-of the-century fictions of female-ness like *She* and *Herland*, post-war classics like *The Sun Also Rises* and *Mrs. Dalloway*, sexual speculations like *Maurice, Orlando*, and *Nightwood*, and fictionalized anthropologies like Lawrence's "The Woman Who Rode Away" and Cather's *The Professor's House*. Finally, we examined theological deconstructions and reconstructions like H.D.'s *Trilogy* and Yeats's *The Death of Cuchulain*, Hurston's *Their Eyes Were Watching God* and West's *Miss Lonelyhearts*.

When we designed our syllabus, we had suspected that there would be a dissonance between male and female responses to crucial socio-historical events like the suffrage movement, World War I, and the entrance of woman into the labor market. We had also anticipated that there would be some discrepancy between male and female experiences of large intellectual happenings like the rise of anthropology and the fall of God. Finally, we knew that men and women would have been differently affected by advances in medical theory and technology that altered infant mortality and marital fertility rates while transforming definitions of female anatomy and destiny. But as we read and reread key modernist texts in relation to these dramatically influential social and intellectual contexts, we found that the literary traces of such different historical experiences were even more marked than we had anticipated. We could only conclude that in the early part of this century men and women had evolved two entirely different versions of the world, visions so different we felt we had to speak not only of male and female modernisms, but of masculinist and feminist modernisms.

In each of the four main areas we studied, for example, we found texts by men that did engage the dramatic feelings of anxiety usually associated with modernism. At the same time, however, we found female texts expressing exuberance at precisely the breakdown of traditional structures that was disturbing male artists. Thus, while H. Rider Haggard's *She* envisions with horror a matriarchal queendom ruled by a fierce 2000-year-old woman called "She-Who-Must-Be-Obeyed," Charlotte Perkins Gilman's *Herland* imagines an all-female country of mothers whose virtues consistently reverse and confound the vices of Haggard's Queen. Similarly, while Hemingway's war-haunted novel *The Sun Also Rises* uses the characters of Jake and Brett to brood on "the horror, the horror" of male impotence and female sexual autonomy, Woolf's novel of post-war England, *Mrs. Dalloway*, emphasizes the ways in which the suicidal fall of Septimus empowers the visionary rise of Clarissa. For, tragic as it is, Septimus's death "made her feel the beauty, made her feel the fun."[2] The generational conflict implicit in the war was, of course, more complicated than such a schema would suggest; writers from Alice Meynell and Katherine Mansfield to Wilfred Owen and Siegfried Sassoon did understand that the slaughter of a whole generation of men in the trenches had set sons bitterly against their fathers. But it was precisely this warping of the pattern of succession upon which patriarchal culture is founded that seems to have instigated a battle of the sexes: as the poet Alice Meynell observed, with the sons gone, the daughters were now the only inheritors left.[3]

Such a demographically striking reversal of genealogical syntax resulted in an obsession not only with sexual experimentation in life, but also in an exploration in literature by both sexes of the third or intermediate sex, of transvestism and of hermaphroditism. Even before the war, of course, E.M. Forster, partly influenced by Edward Carpenter, had begun to long for a male-bonded eroticism that would free men from the stifling parlors and powers of women. But as women gained votes and voices in society, modernists from Joyce and Lawrence to Eliot and Pound started to wonder whether, as Captain A.H. Henderson-Livesey inquired in his book *Sex and Public Life*, "these male-brained, male-voiced, male-imitating, and very often male-hating" creatures could even be called women since their "inverted sex nature is obvious to the veriest tyro."[4] And, indeed, works as diverse as Woolf's *Orlando* and Barnes's *Nightwood* did experiment with the discourse of disguises that one feminist critic, in a somewhat different context, has called "sapphistry."[5]

Inevitably, however, such alternative languages, valorizing female nature and culture, generated self-consciously female mythologies and theologies that were also alarming to men. Thus, while women like Zora Neale Hurston and H.D. dream of male deaths leading to female rebirths, mortal men and immortal women, men like Yeats and West mourn the irrevocable death of the hero slaughtered by or because of the willfulness of revolting women. In *Their Eyes Were Watching God*, for example, Janie's dead lover, Tea Cake, becomes the eucharistic host through which she savours her own salvation, and in H.D.'s *Trilogy*, the ruins of male culture become runes in which the poet reads the message of the goddess who represents her own divinity. Yeats's heroic Cuchulain, on the other hand, is killed by a crow-headed goddess of death, and West's unmanned Miss Lonelyhearts, unable to reach or rouse an absent Christ, falls dead into the waiting arms of a dwarfish "no man." It almost seems as if, in the twentieth-century, the link between violence and the sacred has been reimagined in two very different ways by men and women. With women's shocking entrance into history, men increasingly seem to have felt themselves divorced from what had been their traditional heritage and violently severed from the sacred mythologies that had begotten their legitimacy. The law of the father, they seem to have felt, was being disrupted by the speaking of other tongues: mother tongues.

Two works which particularly address this dissonance between male and female imaginings of violence and the sacred seem to us to be Lawrence's "The Woman Who Rode Away" and Cather's *The Professor's House*. Both stories use the American southwest to reconstruct pre-historic native cultures; both authors see the scene of interaction between civilized and primitive cultures from the perspective of the opposite sex (that is, Lawrence's tale has a female protagonist while Cather's has several male ones); both works were written in the middle twenties when both authors were at the peak of their careers. But, as Kate Millett has noted, nowhere is the violent sacrifice of the sacred female body more theatrically enacted than in Lawrence's story.[6]

To be sure, when his pale nameless heroine first rides away from a technological waste land into a fertile wilderness, Lawrence's sympathies evidently go with her. At thirty-three, she is a proto-typical Christ figure, who seems to have sought the desert in order to desert the past and redeem the future. But when she is captured by a band of strong silent Indians, his feelings appear to divide. At the very moment when his protagonist's will is first violated by these "inscrutable" men who whip her horse against her wishes, Lawrence makes it clear that he is glad she is powerless, glad that "She knew she was dead."[7] As the story progresses, moreover, and its anonymous heroine is moved into a realm of "unearthly glamour" where she is stripped, bathed, anointed, drugged, and bedecked in the ceremonial confines of an ancient men's house, Lawrence exults that "The sharpness and the quivering nervous consciousness of the highly bred white woman was to be destroyed again" (p. 569). His use of the word "again" reminds us of the destruction of another "highly bred white woman" — Mrs. Morel, in *Sons and Lovers*, a portrait of the artist's terrifyingly powerful mother — while the nameless heroine's blonde hair recalls his equally powerful wife, Frieda von Richthofen-Weekley Lawrence. In "The Woman Who Rode Away," however, Lawrence is at last able to convince himself that, almost pornographically, "she wanted it" (p. 577), wanted not only death but quasi-sexual violence.

Interestingly, this complex story seems at certain points to valorize the matriarchal power of the womb, as Lawrence extolls the Indian women who long to "bring the moon back" into the sacred caves of their bodies. Not only, however, do such women never appear in the story, but we are told that they must "get the moon back and keep her *quiet* in their house" [italics ours; p. 571] just so the Indian men can "get the sun and the power over all the world." Finally, then, "The white woman got to die and go like a wind to the sun" (p. 575), so that men can achieve "The mastery that man must hold, and that passes from race to race" (p. 581). Significantly, moreover, the man who achieves that mastery in behalf of his people is an "old, old priest" who plays an increasingly dominant role in the story, a figure out of the unconscious, almost ontologically male in his embodiment of Lawrence's own scenario of sacrificial retribution. "Naked and in a state of barbarous ecstasy" (p. 580), he is the one who must watch "in absolute motionlessness" until the moment "when the red sun," symbolizing maleness, "shall send his ray through the column of ice," symbolizing femaleness. Then, this man of god will "strike, and strike home, accomplish the sacrifice and achieve the power" (p. 581).

Where Lawrence's "The Woman Who Rode Away" mythologizes and mystifies masculinism, Cather's *The Professor's House* attempts to discover and recover a prehistoric civilization whose decline may have been associated with the sacrifice of a woman. At the center of this mystical novel *démeublé* Cather interpolates Tom Outland's story, an adventure tale which describes a young man's archaeological finds in the myth-haunted territories of Cow Canyon, a terrain once inhabited by Pueblo Indians who lived day after day "facing an ocean of clear air."[8] Tracing their way through a deep canyon, Tom Outland and his partner have not been captured but have followed runaway cattle onto an idyllic mesa, where they find intact the ruins and relics of an ancient Cliff City. Here, too, "in a little group of houses stuck up in a high arch we called the Eagle's Nest," they discover what almost seems like the mummified body of the woman who rode away, a murdered woman whom they name Mother Eve:

there was a great wound in her side ... her mouth was open as if she was screaming, and her face, through all those years, had kept a look of terrible agony. (p. 214)

Perhaps, indeed, like Lawrence's heroine, she had been taken to a high mountainous cave to be sacrificed by some priest who "struck and struck home" to achieve "the mastery that man must hold." Certainly her death defines the fall of a culture that was different and, as her name suggests, a paradise lost. For Tom Outland, his friend, and Cather's professorial protagonist, however, that death proposes a possibility of recovery and resurrection, for they soon come to see that "the mesa was no longer an adventure but a religious emotion" (p. 251), a paradise that could perhaps be regained.

Cather's story is, if anything, even more complicated than Lawrence's; the assignment of masculinity to the major characters is only one of the ways in which this ironic and ambivalent author withdraws from the fantasy of female primacy that her archaeological mythmaking often seems to imply. Nevertheless, it is in Cow Canyon that Tom Outland first feels "I had found everything instead of having lost everything" (p. 250). It is here too, cataloging the relics of a people who "possibly declined in the arts of war" (p. 220), so that "they were probably wiped out ... by some roving Indian tribe without ... domestic virtues" (p. 221) that Tom gains the intellectual energy which inspires his discovery of the Outland vacuum, which has "revolutionized aviation." Significantly, when he is killed in World War I, he bequeaths the proceeds of his free-flying dream to the daughter of his old professor. Significantly, too, this aging professor with the quintessentially patriarchal name of St. Peter must reconstruct Tom Outland's narrative about the ancient cliffs and glyphs of Cow Canyon in order to learn how to die.

Just as Tom, in order to confront life, had to recover the prehistoric domesticity of Indians who dwelled among untrodden ways, the professor has to remember his own prepatriarchal self, the boy he was before he became a man and a father, in order to confront death. Renouncing the law of the father that tied him to his family, this disillusioned scholar retreats to an attic furnished with female forms, specifically the dressmaker's dummies used by the family seamstress, Augusta, and in the end it is the fateful and august figure of the spinning spinster who guides him on his spiritual passage out of both life and patriarchy. "Like the taste of bitter herbs," Augusta hasn't "any of the sentimentality that comes from a fear of dying" and "her manner of speaking about it [makes] death seem less uncomfortable" (p. 281). Like Lawrence's priest, she is a hieratic and oneiric, even shamanistic, being, yet she represents not the mastery of men but the mystery of women. Fitting dummies with her intricate patterns of female costumes, Augusta, as the professor concludes, "makes those terrible women" — dummies and mummies alike — "entirely plausible!" (p. 101) When she informs St. Peter that "the Blessed Virgin composed the Magnificat" (p. 100), he thinks of

Queen Mathilde ... doing the long tapestry now shown at Bayeux — working her chronicle of the deeds of knights and heroes[;] alongside the big pattern of dramatic action she and her women carried the little playful pattern of birds and beasts that are a story in themselves. ... (p. 101)

At last, then, when the professor, once the master who propounded the secrets of history to his race, is sacrificed to Augusta's bitter herbs, he "wants" it. No longer "the same man [his wife and daughters] had said goodbye to," he accepts "without delight" but with religious resignation the "bloomless" end Augusta has promised him.

We gained insight into some of these points of comparison and contrast between Lawrence's story and Cather's novel from Anne Jones and Gail Mortimer, two of our seminar participants who had particularly useful ideas about the symbolic import of Augusta's domestic arts and about the transsexual narrative strategies used by both authors, and we have chosen to talk about these two works because the dialectic they embody perfectly reflects the larger inter-sexual dialectic we studied all summer. From the projects of other members of our seminar, however, we gained equally illuminating insights into this dialectical process that seems to us to be central to twentieth-century literary history. In this special issue of *Women's Studies*, all thirteen seminar participants are represented by papers that have been arranged according to the chronology of their subjects. Among them, however, they represent roughly the range of themes we covered in our group-meetings.

Pamela Annas's study of Renée Vivien's poetry, Carole Stone's reading of Kate Chopin's *The Awakening*, and Linda Mizejewski's analysis of Gertrude Stein's *Tender Buttons* all examine women's fantasies of autonomy while exploring the relationship between literary or cultural experimentation and female sensibility. Caryn Musil's reappraisal of Wilfred Owen's verse, Judith Breen's essay on Lawrence's "The Blind Man" and his "Tickets, Please," and Jean Pickering's "On the Battlefield: Vera Brittain's *Testament of Youth*" illuminate the asymmetrical response of men and women to the apocalypse of World War I. Eileen Wiznitzer's study of "Lil" as "the repressed thematic center of *The Waste Land*" explores male modern-ist transformations of sexuality as it uncovers the misogynistic portraits of ladies that T.S. Eliot embedded in his famous poem and meditates on the ways in which a critical discourse that sanitizes such misogyny by claiming its universality infects women with an "anxiety of reading" based on self blame.

Confronting a neglected (rather than a hegemonic) text, Barbara Lootens deals with the intransigence of biological sexuality at the same time that she defines the heroic images and tragic implications that endow a working-class heroine with dignity in Edith Summers Kelley's *Weeds*. Similarly, Jean Wyatt and Melody Zajdel describe uniquely female transformations of sexuality, with Jean Wyatt documenting how the delineation of fluid ego boundaries characterizes Virginia Woolf's *Mrs. Dalloway* and women's fiction in general, and Melody Zajdel tracing the relationship between sexuality and creativity in two of H.D.'s prose works, *Murex* and *Narthex*. Returning to the issue of World War I, Anne Jones compares the divergent reactions of William Faulkner and Katherine Anne Porter to that cultural crisis, while Gail Mortimer, also writing on Faulkner, focuses on the southern novelist's use of vases and urns to represent, on the one hand, the alluring surface, and, on the other hand, the hidden threat, of female sexuality. Finally, Alice Reich explores the sacramental sisterhood that empowers Janie, the heroine of Zora Neale Hurston's *Their Eyes Were Watching God*. Together, then, all these essays recover a history of female modernism that has been ignored or submerged in accounts of twentieth-century literature which focus only on the art of male writers; at the same time, they offer new insights into the way a male-female sexual dialectic impelled the construction of what we have traditionally understood as modernism.

From all this work, we have concluded that the relationship of the female imagination to the modernist aesthetic is indeed of crucial importance, but in a very different way from what we had earlier imagined. Where we had begun by thinking that the connection between women writers and twentieth-century literary history was merely problematic, we now understood that the female imagination was in fact a central problem for modernist men. Thus, to define the woman writer, the way we earlier did, as a prototypical modernist, is, on the one hand, to oversimplify women's literary history, and, on the other hand, to accept hegemonic definitions of modernism which assume the centrality of male texts while desexualizing their contexts.

But what if, as we have now begun to wonder, there is a discontinuity between nineteenth and twentieth-century literature by women that reflects the economic, political, and social release from confinement which women experienced at the turn of the century? Moreover, what if the very existence of nineteenth-century precursors further empowered the writing of twentieth-century women, even as it induced anxiety in their male contemporaries? What if the existence of such a self-valorizing female tradition had to be countered by male self-certification, so that even the emergence of modern male critical discourse — exemplified by works like "Tradition and the Individual Talent," *The ABC of Reading, Studies in Classic American Literature, Seven Types of Ambiguity,* and *The Well-Wrought Urn* — could be seen as an attempt to reconstruct "his" story of a literary history in which women play no part? Perhaps to men like Eliot, Pound, Lawrence, Empson, and Brooks, a literary landscape populated by women writers would have seemed like a "No Man's Land." After all, they may have understood, without articulating the point, what their female contemporaries from Gilman and Cather to Woolf, H. D., and Hurston, always knew: that the woman who rode away from the professor's house wants to live in Herland, a country of her own.

Notes

1.   See Hélène Cixous, "The Laugh of the Medusa," in *New French Feminisms,* ed. Elaine Marks and Isabelle de Courtivron (Amherst: University of Massachusetts Press, 1980); Margaret Homans, *Women Writers and Poetic Identity* (Princeton: Princeton University Press, 1982); Rachel Blau Du Plessis, "For the Etruscans," *The Future of Difference,* ed. Alice Jardine (New York: 1981).
2.   Virginia Woolf, *Mrs Dalloway* (New York: Harcourt, 1925), p. 284.
3.   On generational conflict in World War I, see Sandra M. Gilbert, "Soldier's Heart: Literary men, Literary Women, and the Great War," *Signs: Journal of Women in Culture and Society,* 8, 3 (Spring 1983).
4.   A.H. Henderson-Livesey, *Sex and Public Life* can be read at the Beineke Library.
5.   Jane Marcus, "Liberty, Sorority, Misogyny," in *The Representation of Women in Fiction,* ed. Carolyn Heilbrun and Margaret Higonnet (Baltimore: Johns Hopkins University Press, 1983), pp. 81, 87.
6.   Kate Millet, *Sexual Politics* (New York: Avon, 1969), pp. 376-86.
7.   D.H. Lawrence, *The Complete Short Stories,* Vol. II (New York: Penguin, 1976), p. 556. Subsequent citations will appear parenthetically in the text.
8.   Willa Cather, *The Professor's House* (New York: Vintage, 1973), p. 213. Subsequent citations will appear parenthetically in the text.

"Drunk with chastity":
The poetry of Renée Vivien

PAMELA J. ANNAS

Department of English, University of Massachusetts

You for whom I wrote, oh lovely young women without names,
You whom, alone, I loved, will you reread my verse
On future mornings snowing coldly on the universe,
By future quiet evenings of roses and flames?

Will you sit dreaming, amid the charming disarray
Of dishevelled hair, open robes, of her you never discover
Wherever you look: "Whether on day of mourning or festival day,
This woman wore always her glance, her lips of a lover."

Pale, giving forth a fragrance to haunt my flesh and mind,
In the magic evocation of the night when love should be rare and free
Will you say: "This woman had the ardor I can never find.
What a pity she is not living! She would have loved me!"

("You For Whom I Wrote")[1]

THAT RENÉE VIVIEN addressed her future readers seductively tells us something about her. It also raises the question of what our own relationship is not only to contemporary women writers but to those who have preceded us, especially to a writer like Renée Vivien whose work has been out of print and unavailable in English translation until recently.[2] In what spirit do we, as contemporary feminist readers, enter the text of a woman writer? Are we looking for an oceanic unity of perfect amity where at last we will find a reflection of our own deepest images and desires? Do we harbor a lurking hope that this at last is the text we can dive into safely, a medium that will hold us up and that we don't have to struggle against?

Women's Studies, 1986
Vol. 13, pp. 011-022
0049-7878/86/1302-0011 $18.50/0

If such is the case, and I detect such a yearning in myself from time to time, then we are bound to be not only bemused, interested, and delighted to recover another lost woman writer but also startled, disappointed, and sometimes threatened when we inevitably discover differences between our own vision and the writer's — as we are certain to do when we read Renée Vivien's poetry. Most of us have by now developed the prickly survival skills of Judith Fetterley's resisting reader.[3] But since literature by its nature invites us to let down our defenses as we cross its borders, and since we have been trained to accept this invitation, it tends to be a relief for a reader exhausted from trying to find a reasonable facsimile of herself in works by male writers to relax into the warm embrace of the female text. However, the unresisting reader of female texts encounters a set of problems as potent as, though different from, the problem encountered by Fetterley's resisting reader of male-authored texts.

The contemporary feminist reader of Renée Vivien's poetry is likely to be both attracted and repelled as she crosses its borders, attracted by the woman-identified world Vivien writes about and the primacy of women's relationships within it, repelled by its turn-of-the century decadence and by its ambiance of languishing lesbians and wilting lilies, of artificiality and death. As in reading the work of another twentieth-century poet who skirmished with self-destruction, Sylvia Plath, we cannot identify with Renée Vivien's world too thoroughly because in part the contradictions embodied in the poetry lead to a denial of life. On another level, we cannot read Renée Vivien primarily from the perspective of the mores and politics of our own time. To do this is to misread her and perhaps to dismiss her too hastily. While we might be able to see the work of *contemporary* women poets as "an arena into which we enter to change ourselves and each other,"[4] how do we approach this poetry from the first decade of the twentieth century as more than an exotic and anachronistic lesbian artifact? The reader of Renée Vivien's verse needs to be both engaged and detached enough to recognize the contradictions Renée Vivien lived, made mythic structures out of, and built into her art.

She was one of the first twentieth-century lesbian poets. Lesbian poetry has been, in the twentieth century, explicitly political poetry, romantic love poetry, poems which explain or assume the complexities and realities of lesbian relationships, poems of definition and discovery, erotic poetry, poems by lesbians not explicitly about lesbian experience, and closet or coded poetry. Renée Vivien's poetry is coded, even though it is consciously lesbian poetry — erotic, romantic, about some of the complexities of women's relationships as she saw them, occasionally explicitly political — a poetry that celebrates lesbian experience, but more than celebrates, accepts it as a given. San Giovanni, the Androgyne who is the mythic hero of Vivien's novel, *A Woman Appeared to Me*, says: "I neither love nor hate men. . . . What I hold against them is the great wrong they have done to women. They are political adversaries whom I want to injure for the good of the cause. Off the battlefield of ideas, I know them little and am indifferent to them."[5]

By categorizing lesbian poetry in this way, I do not at all mean to diminish it, though I do want to raise the question of how "free" a gay or lesbian writer is to write about other things than being gay or lesbian in a world that defines them as deviant. It was in Renée Vivien's lifetime, in the late nineteenth and history as a named separate group.[6] Much as woman becomes hero in the twentieth century precisely because, as Carolyn Heilbrun remarks, woman's situation is characteristic of the generic twentieth-century individual,[7] the homosexual artist's position as defined other is emblematic of a historical period that has seen the birth of psychology, the loss of individual identity as a given, and the consequent necessity to construct one's identity from moment to moment, to make fairly conscious choices about who one is, to feel simultaneously a sense of possibility and a fear that there is no self, to feel inside oneself an outsider. Renée Vivien's alienated status was multifold: as a woman who wanted to write, as a lesbian who wanted to be so openly, as an American/British expatriate in Paris, as a writer who chose not to write in her own language, as a person who literally took on a new name and identity. On the other hand, we can say that she came to Paris to be inside and unalienated — to live as a lesbian, to write from that experience, to be read sympathetically. As a member of an outgroup, Renée Vivien necessarily wrote in tension with the world that defined her as marginal and outside the norm, and that tension helped to shape, conceal, and inform her poetry.

Lesbian poetry in the twentieth century has been, by definition, an outlaw literature.[8] Renée Vivien's life and work have implications for the study of more well known twentieth-century writers. She was, for example, one of the first twentieth-century expatriates; and the act of expatriation — of deliberately alienating, estranging, ungrounding oneself in order to write — is characteristic of much modern literature. What are the distinctions between, and what are the connections among, being an expatriate, an exile, and an outlaw? Is the stance of outsider based on choice, on whether or not you can go back? Is it based on the writer's attitude toward herself and her subject in the new place? Many expatriates wrote about the lives they had left; Renée Vivien wrote only about the life she was living and she wrote about that obliquely. Chosen or not, irrevocable or not, how does a writer handle, in her life and art, the fact of being the other? Renée Vivien's art is powered by contradictions she lived and never fully resolved: tensions between denial and affirmation, between being hidden and being open, between unnaming and renaming herself and her world.

Before she literally renamed herself, Renée Vivien was Pauline Tarn (born 1877), a young woman of British and American parentage who had been to school in France and formed an intense, emotionally passionate but physically chaste friendship with Violet Shilleto (Ione in Vivien's *roman a clef*, *A Woman Appeared to Me*). From age 16 to 20, Pauline lived, unhappily with her parents in England, the life of an upper-class young lady. At age 21, Pauline Tarn talked her parents into letting her live in Paris, where she promptly became Renée Vivien and soon met Natalie Barney, the Vally of *A Woman Appeared to Me* and the subject of many of Vivien's poems. The relationship was stormy from the beginning, in part (and ostensibly) because Barney believed in having many love affairs and Vivien wanted only Barney. Barney, often referred to in the French literary world as "the Amazon," made an art form and a religion of sensual paganism and lived to be 96 (1876-1972). Her many love affairs included Liane de Pougy, Dolly Wilde, and a 50 year long relationship with the painter Romaine Brooks, who also lived to be 96 (1874-1970).[9] Vivien, on the other hand, drank and starved herself to death by 1909 at the age of 31. Between 1899 and 1909, however, she wrote approximately eighteen volumes of poetry and prose. When Violet Shilleto, Vivien's early love who had introduced her to Barney, died (young) in 1901, Vivien and Barney broke up, and Vivien began a relationship with the Baronness Helen Van Zuylen de Nyevelt (née Rothschild). In 1904, Renée Vivien and Natalie Barney reunited briefly and sailed to Mytilene, the Isle of Sappho, with the intention of reestablishing a lesbian circle there. The Baronness broke up this idyll, but it was a pivotal event for Vivien's poetry. Details of the last few years of Renée Vivien's life are hard to find. She was increasingly ill from drug abuse and slow starvation. And although she had embraced paganism all her adult life, imagining herself reborn not into a Christian afterlife but into Lesbos, where Sappho "will show us, in her graceful manner,/ The Lesbian orchard that opens to the sea" ("Like This Would I Speak," SB), she converted to Catholicism three days before she died.[10]

Renée Vivien/Pauline Tarn's life and poetry are built on contradiction. Like Sylvia Plath, whose poetry also emerges from contradiction, Vivien killed herself by age 31. Hers was the more subtle suicide of anorexia and alcoholism. Though death imagery is characteristic of the poetry of both these women, neither poet is simply working out a death wish in her verse. Sylvia Plath's strongest poems ("Daddy," "Lady Lazarus," "Tulips," "Ariel") point *through* death toward the rebirth of a transformed self into a transformed world.[11] Renée Vivien's death imagery is attributable in part to her use of the French Symbolist tradition. The imagery of her poems mirrors the contradictions of her life; it is drawn from two opposing literary models of being a lesbian: the Baudelairean or life-denying and the Sapphic or life-affirming. The Symbolist and Sapphic modes both at least admitted the existence of the lesbian and were therefore immediately appropriate and accessible to a young lesbian poet at the turn-of-the-century. They were potential models upon which to structure an art and an identity, even though neither had much to do with history and with life as it is lived day to day. The atmosphere of artificiality ("To be as different as possible from Nature is the true function of Art," says Vally in *A Woman Appeared to Me*[12]) and the grotesque, the image of the *femme fatale*, the images of death and darkness in Vivien's poetry are consciously Baudelairean: "your voice — a treacherous tide;/ Your arms — supple reeds,/ Long river reeds, their embrace/ Enlaces, chokes, strangles savagely" ("Undine," *Études et Préludes*, CK).

"Velleity" (*Cendres et Poussieres*, 1902, MP) captures the contradiction that characterizes much of Renée Vivien's poetry. That tension first appears in the title. "Velleity" means volition in its weakest form or a mere wish, unaccompanied by an effort to obtain it.

Loosen your feverish arms, oh my mistress, dismiss
Me. Set me free from the yoke of your bitter kiss.
Far from your lascivious, oppressive scent,
Far from the languours of the bed where our hours are spent,

On the breath of the wind I shall breathe the sharp salt air,
The acrid tang of the algae; till clean and bare,
I shall go towards the wild profundity of the sea,
Pale from solitude, drunk with chastity.

The words and images of the first stanza evoke both entrapment and a wish to escape: "loosen," "set me free," "yoke," "oppressive," "far from," and "mistress," implying slave.[13] The first stanza of "Velleity" is representative of a type of poem for which Renée Vivien is probably best known — about a bitter love, unrequited, insatiate, exotic, erotic, suffocating, and vaguely evil. The second stanza opens out. The images (and the reader) breathe more freely — sharp salt air and acrid tang rather than "lascivious oppressive scent," energy and movement rather than langour, "wild profundity" rather than "feverish arms," as we move toward the "pale solitude" of the final line. The poem is in part about a recovery of one's self from the self-loss of passion. But though the poem's end celebrates solitude, it also, in the phrase "drunk with chastity," looks back to the feverish arms in the opening line and to the title's suggestion of an inability to let go. It doubles back upon itself and remains entangled in its own contradictions.

"Chastity" and "virginity" in Vivien's poetry explicitly refer to lesbian sexuality. In "Love Poem" (*Les Kitharedes*, CK), she writes:

Your eyes stabbed me with a double flame;
I saw you, lovely woman! and mused on
your virgin face and your womanly thighs.

In "I Will Stay Virgin" (*Sappho*, CK), it is clear that virginity does not mean sexual abstinance or inexperience but rather freedom from *male* sexual desire, which she describes as "the horrible embrace,/ And the corroding kiss." The poet chooses Diana over Apollo, the virgin moon over "the brutal sun." The last lines of this poem are lovely and affirming.

I will stay virgin like the moon
Reflected in the glass tide
Troubled by the long sigh of desire
            For the ocean

But the operative word here is "troubled." Even within the relationships between women which she celebrates, Vivien indicates a holding back, a desire which is disturbing but unconsummated, which allows one no peace but is nevertheless not acted on, a mere wish, unaccompanied by an effort to obtain it. This tension is especially characteristic of Vivien's early poetry.

The contradictions in Renée Vivien's life are probably best captured in Colette's vivid portrait of her in *The Pure and the Impure*. We need to read this cautiously, for Colette admits she is not all that sympathetic to Vivien: "Like all those who never use their strength to the limit, I am hostile to those who let life burn them out."[14]

There is not a single feature of her youthful face that I do not vividly recall. Everything in it bespoke childishness, roguishness, and the propensity to laughter. Impossible to find anywhere in that face, from the fair hair to the sweet dimple of the weak little chin, any line that was not a line of laughter, any sign of the hidden tragic melancholy that throbs in the poetry of Renée Vivien. I never saw Renée sad.[15]

In contrast, Colette remembers Vivien in her Paris apartment: "Among the unstable marvels, Renée wandered, not so much clad as veiled in black or purple, almost invisible in the scented darkness of the immense rooms barricaded with leaded windows, the air heavy with curtains and incense."[16] It is this atmosphere which is so initially off-putting to a contemporary reader. One feels stifled, like Colette who tried one day to open a window in Vivien's apartment and found it nailed shut.

However, though Renée Vivien furnished her apartment in *fin de siècle* opium-den opulence, she also traveled with Natalie Barney to Sappho's Mytilene, the Isle of Lesbos, a place that in her poetry represents the fantasy memory of open spaces, innocence, a sunny sensuality, freedom, and the Golden Age.

> — a virgin with a sweet voice.
> I listen, dreaming. Your refreshing voice
>   Runs like the water of a spring over moss,
>   Appeasing my old sorrows, my persistent loss.
> In your virgin sweetness I rejoice.

> Eros today has torn my soul,
>   wind which is the mountain
>   fells the oaks.
> Eros has bent my soul with giant strokes
> As a mountain wind twists and breaks great oaks ...
> And I see perish in the fire's moving light
>   A whole moth flight.

Vivien's themes of loss, grief, and death are not absent from these meditations on Sappho, but the images in which the conflict is expressed are natural rather than artificial.

Until approximately 1904, there are two opposite clusters of imagery in Renée Vivien's poetry; the life-denying images are associated with the French Symbolist tradition with which Vivien was quite familiar; the life-affirming images are associated with Sappho's poetry, which Vivien learned Greek to translate. On the one hand, there is suffering, unfulfilled desire, death, violets and lilies, the artificial, shadows, lust, that which is cunning, artful, designing, colors which are dark, dull or wan, tombs, transience, tangled nets, water to drown in, weeping, dependence, weary decadence, sickness, frailty and faintness, whores, the corrosive and tainted, cruelty, spring, especially April, anxiety, night, perfume, being trapped, drugs, the drowned or dying lady, one's self as victim or slave. On the other hand, there is joy, exquisitely fulfilled desire, life, ripening apples, roses, summer grass, anemones, thyme, fennel, hyacinth, the natural, sunshine, sunsets and flames, desire and affection, the open, simple and passionate, colors which are bright and shining, amber, gold, purple, meadows, transcendence of time, beehives, water that is fresh and refreshing, laughter, independence, childlike innocence, health, virginity, snow and purity, gentleness and tenderness, summer, autumn, and winter, peace, daytime, sea air, freedom, magic, strong

women, goddesses, and female power. Images of serpents and pale-
ness, particular to Renée Vivien's poetry, and other images that I
think of as characteristically women's images — the moon, mirrors
and reflections, trees, the ocean — appear in both worlds.

The poems from 1904 on — after Vivien's trip to Mytilene and her
final break with Barney — move out of both these extremes into
images that are less fevered, less literary and, relatively speaking, more
about everyday life and real people and emotions.

You love the brown-eyed autumn and the clatter
Of doors where the wind leaves a salty taste:
You spin, by the song of your humble wheel,
      The snowy flax.

The virgin respects and fears your wisdom,
And your greetings are slow like a good-bye,
Whitehaired women, flowers of old age,
      You who speak little. ...

Though as a paeon to age, "Whitehaired Women" (*Les Kitharedes*,
CK) is still a romanticized portrait, it is nonetheless an "objective"
poem in the sense that its subject is outside the poet; its mood is
calmer, its atmosphere more homey than exotic. In "Sappho Lives
Again" (*A l'heure des mains jointes*, SB), the tone is anything but weary
decadence: "We women love with an infinite candor,/With the
amazement of an astonished child/For whom a whole new world has
opened up ..." The title poem from *At the Sweet Hour of Hand in Hand*
has this statement of convalesence moving toward health as its central
stanza:

Your hair, your voice, your arms have healed me.
I have cast off fear and brutal suspicion
I have shed the artificial and the bizarre ...
I shelter my heart from a long sickness
Recovering slowly under your healing roof.

In "Pilgrimage" (*Haillons*, CK), one of Vivien's last poems before her
death in 1909, she writes, with a new openness,

It seems as if I have neither sex nor age,
My troubles have so abruptly overcome me.
Time has woven itself ... And here I am barefooted,
Finishing the terrible and long pilgrimage. ...

Karla Jay advances four reasons why Renée Vivien (and Natalie Barney, also an expatriate) wrote in French: 1) her education was bilingual. Vivien spent time in France between the ages of seven and thirteen and by the time she was sixteen was already writing parts of her diary in French. 2) Vivien's poetic masters, except Swinburne and Shakespeare (and, of course, Sappho) were French — Baudelaire, Verlaine, Mallarmé. She used French metrics. 3) She came to Paris to be part of a literary tradition, Symbolism, which had been articulated primarily in French. 4) The French language and a Paris audience were temperamentally better suited to both Vivien and Barney than English language or an English or American audience would have been. Barney said that it was natural they wrote in a language not their own and died in a country they weren't born in.[17]

Though Renée Vivien apparently wrote consciously and openly from within her early twentieth-century lesbian world, she wrote through a series of buffers and within a series of frames. *A Woman Appeared to Me*, for example, is a coded novel about a real love affair and real people which contains as its central character a mythological character called The Androgyne who relates an interpolated story which has been told to her by a nameless adventurer. Similarly, in the Sappho poems, an epigraph from Sappho is translated from the Greek into French by Renée Vivien, who is actually the British/American Pauline Tarn. This is followed by a free meditation on the fragment by Vivien, in French. Finally, as English and American readers, we have had to wait some 70 years to read the poems in Vivien's native language. Though she writes a love poem to her future readers, though she imagines us recoding her verse "On future mornings snowing coldly on the universe,/By future quiet evenings of roses and flames," still there is a lot of distance between the contemporary reader and this woman who chose to write intimate poems in a language not her own. Add to this Vivien's tendency to filter experience through the literary conventions of Symbolist and Sapphic verse and, as readers, we have an unusually complex relationship to a poet whose own relation to her self, her subject, her medium, and her audience(s) was unusually problematic. Renée Vivien's writing remains for us both accessible and hidden. If she ever resolved the contradictions and the tension in her life and poetry, she did so by being simultaneously self-revelatory and masked.

Notes

1. Renée Vivien, *At the Sweet Hour of Hand in Hand* (Naiad Press, 1979), translated by Sandia Belgrade. Also in English translation is *The Muse of the Violets* (Naiad Press, 1977), translations by Margaret Porter and Catharine Kroger of poems from the range of Vivien's work. (Subsequently, the translator will be indicated in the text by initials.) Karla Jay is working on a new translation of Renée Vivien's poems. In French: 1902 — *Cendres et poussieres*; *Brumes de fjords*. 1903 — *Sappho*; *Du vert au violet*; *Evocations*; *La Venus des aveugles*. 1904 — *Etudes et preludes*; *Kitharedes*; *La dame a la louve*; *Aphrodite et M. Pepin*; *Le Christ*; *Une femme m'apparut.* 1906 — *A l'heure des mains jointes.* 1908 — *Sillages*; *Flambeaux eteints.* 1910 — *Dans un coin de violettes*; *Le vent des vaisseaux*; *Haillons.* 1934 — *Poesies completes*, I & II.

2. I am not approaching Renée Vivien's poems as a scholar of French poetry and have therefore worked primarily with translations. My own interest is in Vivien's place in a radical tradition of twentieth century American/British women poets.

3. Judith Fetterley, *The Resisting Reader: A Feminist Approach to American Fiction* (Bloomington, Ind.: Indiana University Press, 1978).

4. Nancy Jo Hoffman, "Reading Women's Poetry: The Meaning and Our Lives," *College English* 34 (October 1972), pp. 48-62.

5. Renée Vivien, *A Woman Appeared to Me*, translated by Jeannette H. Foster (Naiad Press, 1979), p. 8.

6. Gayle Rubin, in her introduction to *A Woman Appeared to Me*, writes: "the 'new' gay history is characterized by the insight that 'however people have behaved sexually throughout European history, they did not live in a world of heterosexuals and homosexuals until quite recently,'" [Bert Hansen, in a review of Jeffrey Weeks' *Coming Out* (Quartet, London, 1977)] "The object of the new gay history is to describe, date, and explain the emergence of this world of sexually specialized persons and its concomitant sociology and politics. While the periodization is by no means settled, there is a growing consensus among gay historians that this modern sexual system was consolidated in or by the last two decades of the nineteenth century in western Europe." (p. xxii)

7. Carolyn Heilbrun, *Toward a Recognition of Androgyny* (New York: Harper & Row, 1973)

8. For a further discussion of this point see Elly Bulkin, "Kissing Against the Light: A look at Lesbian Poetry," *Radical Teacher* #10 (December 1978), pp. 7 - 17.

9. Arlene Raven, "The Eye of the Be*Hold*Her: The Lesbian Vision of Romaine Brooks," *Sinister Wisdom* #16 (Spring 1981), pp. 35-42. For biographical information on Pauline Tarn/Renée Vivien (and her place in the Paris Lesbian Circle)

see also Jean Chalon, *Portrait of a Seductress: The World of Natalie Barney* (New York: Crown, 1979); Colette, *The Pure and the Impure* (1932; rpt., New York: Farrar, Straus & Giroux, 1966); Lillian Faderman, *Surpassing the Love of Men* (New York: William Morrow, 1981); Jeannette Foster, *Sex Variant Women in Literature* (New York: Vantage, 1956); Gayle Rubin, the introduction to *A Woman Appeared to Me*, pp. iii-xxii; George Wickes, *The Amazon of Letters: The Life and Loves of Natalie Barney* (New York: G.P. Putnam's Sons, 1976).

10.   It helps put the Paris Lesbian Circle into perspective if one remembers that 1898, the year Pauline/Renée moved to Paris, was the same year that Charlotte Perkins Gilman published her socialist feminist treatise, *Women and Economics*, in which she asserts that the economic independence of women is a necessary precondition of other kinds of freedom. Many of the lesbians in Paris at the turn of the century and later, including Gertrude Stein, were wealthy women. Natalie Barney inherited a fortune of two million dollars. Renée had what Natalie called a modest income, such that she couldn't furnish a new apartment and take a trip to America at the same time, but enough to live on comfortably. Certainly she had the independent income and a room of her own which Virginia Woolf has said is requisite for literary creation.

11.   Pamela Annas, "The Self in the World: The Social Context of Sylvia Plath's Late Poems" in *Women's Studies: An Interdisciplinary Journal*, Vol. 7, Nos. 1/2 (1980), pp. 171-183.

12.   Renée Vivien, *A Woman Appeared to Me*, p. 14.

13.   In *A Woman Appeared to Me*, the first person narrator refers to herself and is referred to by others as the "slave" of her lover, Vally.

14.   Colette, *The Pure and the Impure*, p. 97.

15.   Ibid., p. 80.

16.   Ibid., p. 81.

17.   Karla Jay, "The Lesbian Expatriates: Barney, Vivien, Stein," a paper read at the Modern Language Association Convention, 1981.

The female artist in Kate Chopin's *The Awakening*: Birth and creativity

CAROLE STONE

Verona, New Jersey

WHEN KATE CHOPIN's *The Awakening* was published in 1899 critics attacked its depiction of a heroine who sought sexual pleasure outside of marriage and condemned Chopin for "failing to perceive that the relation of a mother to her children is far more important than the gratification of a passion which experience has taught her is . . . evanescent."[1] But *The Awakening* is even more radical in its treatment of motherhood because it questions the assumptions that childbirth and child care are a woman's principal vocation, and that motherhood gives pleasure to all women.

In Chopin's era childbirth was considered a woman's noblest act; to write of it otherwise was unacceptable. Thus, the clinical details of pregnancy and birthing remained largely unwritten. As Dr. Mandelet tells Edna in *The Awakening*. "The trouble is that youth is given up to illusions. It seems to be a provision of Nature to secure mothers for the race."[2] But Dr. Mandelet's insight is rare for a man because he is a physician. By shattering the illusion that giving birth is a glorious experience, Chopin attacks the patriarchal structure which denies women control of their bodies. In addition, however, she goes beyond naturalism in her use of the birth motif. On the symbolic level birthing is a metaphor for the rebirth of the book's protagonist, Edna Pontellier, as artist. The novel can be read as a depiction of the growth of the

Women's Studies, 1986
Vol. 13, pp. 023-032
0049-7878/86/1302-0023 $18.50/0

female artist, a *bildungsroman*, in which birth is emphasized as unique to the female experience.

Many recent critics of *The Awakening* fail to see Edna's growing sense of power and control as signs of progress toward a new self-definition. They view her as a woman deluded by romanticism who is unable to make a conscious choice, such as the decision to become an artist, because her instincts are regressive. Cynthia Griffin Wolff, for example, considers Edna passive, an artist at the mercy of her work. Further, she finds that for Edna birth is a pyschic trauma awakening her to the impossibility of total fusion with another.[3] Another critic, Suzanne Wolkenfeld, considers that Edna's "experience of rebirth is not directed toward new life, but backward to the womb."[4] And James Justus observes that Edna's "awakening is not an advance towards a new definition of self but a return to the protective self-evident identity of childhood,"[5] while Donald A. Ringe considers Edna's romanticism part of a voyage of transcendental self-discovery, but concludes that Chopin "allows her character no limitless expansion of self."[6] A more recent critic, Carole Christ, views Edna's awakening in a positive light, seeing her evolving sense of self as spiritual rebirth. However, Christ, too, finds Edna ultimately socially defeated in spite of the very important fact that this heroine grows as an artist.[7]

In this essay I will argue that Edna's memories of her childhood, her immersion in the sea, and her search for a mother figure are emblems of regression in the service of progression toward an artistic vocation. Rather than returning to the dependency of childhood, she goes forward to a new conception of self, a definition of herself as artist. Further, I will suggest that Edna's romanticism is positive because it catalyzes her imaginative power. As the final step forward functioning as an autonomous human being, moreover, she sees through the delusion of romantic love after confronting the horror of giving birth.

Edna's artistic birthing is shown through the contrasting characters of two women, Adèle Ratignolle, a "mother-woman," and Mme. Reisz, a pianist. As Per Seyersted has observed, "the novel covers two generations and births ... a finely wrought system of tensions and interrelations set up between Edna's slow birth as authentic and sexual being and the counterpointed pregnancy and confinement of Adèle."[8] Adèle embodies female biology, always talking of her condition, for she has a baby about every two years. Adèle's opposite, Mme. Reisz, a serious artist, is unmarried. She exemplifies the solitary life of the dedicated artist.

A third influence on Edna's artistic development is Robert LeBrun, a young Creole man who, because he has not yet assumed the masculine values of his society, can be a friend to Edna as her husband cannot. He teaches her to swim, furthering her autonomy, and with his easy way of talking about himself, encourages her self-expression. Because he has aroused sexual desire in her, she eventually has an affair with another man, Alcée Arobin, an affair which functions as a rite of passage to sexual autonomy.

Each of these three figures has positive and negative qualities that help and hinder Edna's struggle to be creative. Adèle Ratignolle, a sensuous woman, awakes Edna to the sensuality of her own body. Also Adèle's candor in talking about such subjects as her pregnancy helps Edna to overcome her reserve. Furthermore, Adèle encourages her to express thoughts and feelings she had kept hidden, even from herself. For example, at Adèle's urging to say what she is thinking as they sit together by the sea, Edna recalls "a summer day in Kentucky, of a meadow that seemed as big as the ocean to the very little girl . . . She threw out her arms as if swimming when she walked, beating the tall grass as one strikes out in the water." (17) When Edna says that she feels as if this summer is like walking through that meadow again "unguided," Adèle strokes her hand, and we see that in fact, though not an artist, it is she who guides Edna toward warmth, openness, and creativity. For Edna's memory is an important step in the growth of her power of free association, necessary in the creative process.

In these early scenes by the sea Chopin also establishes the sea as a central symbol for Edna's birthing of a new self. The connection in her mind between the grass and the sea foreshadows the autonomy she achieves by learning to swim, as well as her final walk into the sea at the book's end. Symbolically, the sea is both a generative and a destructive force in *The Awakening*; it represents danger inherent in artistic self-expression — losing oneself in unlimited space — as well as the source of all life, facilitating rebirth, so that Edna in her first moments of being able to swim feels like a child who has learned to walk. The ocean has also been seen as a symbol of woman or the mother in both her benevolent and terrible aspects. Madame Ratignolle, in association with the sea, represents the benevolent mother who nurtues Edna and even inspires her to paint. Adèle seems to her, as she is seated on the beach, like "some sensuous Madonna," and she paints her picture.

At this beginning point in her artistic development Edna thinks of herself as a "dabbler." However, though Edna has had no formal training, Chopin establishes the fact that she is talented for "she handled her brushes with a certain ease and freedom which came not from a long and close acquaintance with them but from a natural aptitude." (12) We also see early on that Edna has the capacity for self-criticism as "after surveying the sketch critically, she drew a broad smudge of paint across its surface and crumpled the paper between her hands." (12) Later when Edna's critical faculties are turned against conventional values of home, husband, and family in the direction of autonomy, Adèle will show the negative side of her mothering qualities. By constantly reminding Edna of her duty to her children, she binds her to society's rules and impedes her creative growth.

In these early scenes at Grand Isle where Edna's struggle to be an artist is beginning, Robert is another source of imaginative power. As she paints Adèle's portrait, he encourages her with "expressions of appreciation in French." While this may simply be Creole flattery, it is more encouragement than she has ever received from her husband. Like Adèle, he is sensual, and as she paints he rests his head against her arm. He also speaks about himself freely, telling her of his plans to go to Mexico. Under his influence she speaks to him about her life, and it is he who awakens her to the passions of her body. A few weeks after the painting scene on the beach, Chopin again uses the sea as a symbol of growth, and again in connection with Robert. One evening he proposes a night swim and we see him lingering behind with the lovers, "and there was not one but was ready to follow when he led the way." (28) Robert's appearance is associated frequently with lovers; he becomes Cupid who awakens Edna to the force of Eros. This evening she learns to swim and feels herself "reaching out for the unlimited in which to lose herself." (30) Loss of boundaries suggests orgiastic union which foreshadows Edna's final merging with the sea.

Significantly, that evening as she lies in a hammock, an image of lovemaking, she feels herself "pregnant with the first felt throbbing desire" (32) for Robert.

When her husband returns later she refuses to go inside when he asks her to. By now she has achieved mastery over her body by learning to swim and mastery over her environment by challenging his authority. She now has to achieve mastery over her imagination, but at this point can only "blindly follow whatever impulse moved her." (34) Next morning, without much thought, she asks a servant to tell Robert she wishes him to take the boat with her to Cheniere for Mass. Walking to the wharf, there are, as always when Robert appears, lovers who already stroll "shoulder to shoulder." Edna's imagination is subsumed by the romance phase of her creative growth as she spends an idyllic day with Robert. This chapter could be considered an epithalamion which, like Edmund Spenser's, is governed by the position of the sun during each part of the marriage day. On the boat trip, "The lovers were all along. They saw nothing, they heard nothing." (36) Edna and Robert became like the lovers, infatuated with each other, as the sun was high up and beginning to bite." (36)

Edna grows tired in church during Mass, and we see her reject another of society's institutions of authority in favor of the natural force of Eros. Robert takes her to the home of Madame Antoine where Edna partially removes her clothes and while Robert waits for her outside, lies down "in a strange, quaint bed, with its country odor of the laurel, lingering about the sheets and mattress." (39) The laurel, expressive of victory and celebration, is a tree sacred to Apollo, and since the sun charts the course of this harmonious day, the association is clear. The festival being celebrated is a mock wedding, and the hammock which Edna slept in the night before has been replaced by the marriage bed.

Edna wakes to an Edenic world of simple pleasure and magical properties. Beside her bed are bread and wine, symbolizing communion. Outside she picks an orange from a tree in a natural paradise where, Robert tells her, she has slept for a hundred years while he guarded her. As the day ends they watch the sun "turning the western sky to flaming copper and gold," (41) as Madame Antoine tells them stories. She represents the oral tradition of art, a simple phase which Edna can enjoy and emulate. On the boat trip back, Edna hears "the whispering voices of dead men and the click of muffled gold." (42) This day is the high point of romance in Edna's imagination, and she will return to it in her memory as she paints, and as she repeats Madame Antoine's stories.

The woman who represents a structured form of art is Mme. Reisz, the true artist Edna wishes to become. While Madame Ratignolle plays the piano solely for the pleasure of her family, Mme. Reisz plays Frederic Chopin with great feeling and art. Before hearing Mme. Reisz play, music had evoked pictures in Edna's mind. After listening to her play, Edna's passions are aroused. But like such nineteenth century female artists as Emily Dickinson, Mme. Reisz is unmarried, childless, eccentric in manner and in dress, and alienated from society. She cannot serve as a role model for Edna. Nevertheless, Edna's creative development continues. After the family's return to New Orleans, she takes up her painting once more in spite of her husband's admonishment that she "not let the family go to the devil" while she paints. She works with "great energy and interest" though she feels she is not accomplishing anything. Often she sings "Ah tu savais," the song Robert sang on Grand Isle, and she recalls:

the ripple of the water, the flapping sail. She could see the glint of the moon upon the bay, and could feel the soft, gusty beating of the hot south wind. A subtle current of desire passed through her body, weakening her hold upon the brushes and making her eyes burn. (62)

On the one hand romance limits her work, but on the other hand it is a source of inspiration.

There are factors beyond Edna's control, however, which limit her development. Gilbert and Gubar, in a discussion of the woman writer in patriarchal society, describe "the loneliness of the female artist, her feelings of alienation from male predecessors coupled with her need for sisterly precursors and successors, her urgent need for a female audience."[9] Certainly this describes Edna's situation as she seeks out her two contrasting women friends for validation, Mme. Reisz and Adèle Ratignolle. She brings her paintings to Adèle even though she knows in advance, "her opinion in such a matter would be next to valueness ... but she sought the words of praise and encouragement that would help her to put heart into her venture." (59) Adèle, true to her character as a "mother-woman," tells her that her talent is immense, and Edna is pleased even though she recognizes "its true worth." She receives a much harsher judgement of her artistic capacity from Mme. Reisz. In reply to the question of what she has been doing, Edna tells her "I am becoming an artist" and her friend says, "Ah! an artist. You have pretensions, Madame." (68) Sensing the insecurity which keeps her from total commitment to art, Mme. Reisz warns, "To be an artist includes much; one must possess many gifts — absolute gifts — which have not been acquired by one's own effort. And moreover, to succeed the artist must possess the courageous soul." (68)

But there is much evidence to show the growth in Edna's capacity to be an artist. She is learning to enjoy solitude, and her teacher, an art dealer, observes that her work "grows in force and individuality." At a dinner party she tells the Baratarian story she heard from Madame Antoine, and her imagination has grown so much that she makes "every glowing word seem real" to her listeners. Shortly after, she moves out of her husband's house, using money from an inheritance and from the sale of her paintings, into a smaller house of her own. Edna's little house, like Woolf's "room of one's own," is a symbol for growing psychic and financial independence. In addition, even more important than these actions, Edna has defined herself as an artist. Jokingly she says to Mme. Reisz, "You see that I have persistence. Does that quality count for anything in art?" (68) Indeed it does. Edna paints even though she lacks the serious criticism from others that could help her shape her art and despite the fact that she misses the support of women artists who understand the special obstacles that impede female creativity.

Two events occur almost simultaneously at the novel's climax, events which portray the forces that finally defeat Edna's search for artistic wholeness. One is her witnessing of Adèle's suffering in childbirth and the other is Robert's admitting that he loves her and wants to marry her. Edna has gone to Adèle, leaving Robert just after he tells her he has dreamed of marrying her if her husband will free her. She has replied that she is no longer one of Mr. Pontellier's possessions to be given away. When she returns from Adèle's he is gone, having explained in a note that he has left not because he doesn't love her but because he does. Robert has been deeply connected to her sexual growth, which in turn affected the growth of her imagination. Through him she has begun to transfer the authenticity of her romantic vision to her paintings. Now, romantic illusions shattered, she loses the catlyst for her art.

The other illusion that is shattered is that of childbirth being a moment of joy. Edna does not remember her own pain when she gave birth, since she was chloroformed. Now, seeing Adèle's pain, she recognizes that she cannot rebel against nature. Adèle's parting words "think of the children" remind her of her mother-role which conflicts with her new-found freedom. Chopin was far ahead of her time in exposing the myth of bearing children as a woman's ultimate fulfillment, calling Adèle's "acouchement" a scene of torture. Almost a century later Sylvia Plath was to use the same image in *The Bell Jar* by describing the delivery room as "some awful torture chamber."[10] And a doctor tells Plath's protagnist Esther, just as Dr. Mandelet told Edna, "They oughtn't to let women watch. You'll never want a baby if you do. It'll be the end of the human race."[11]

The next morning Edna returns to Grand Isle and walks to her death in the sea. Is her suicide triggered by Adèle's suffering in childbirth? By the knowledge that it is futile to rebel against biology? Does she kill herself because Robert has left her? Or because she has failed to become an artist? Edna drowns herself because she cannot live as a conventional wife or mother any longer, and society will not accept her newfound self. The solitude she enjoys makes for artistic growth, but she is bound to children, home, social duty. She will not sacrifice her new autonomy because, as Anne Jones points out, "she will not relinquish the core of her vision, which is not finally romance, but rather her own autonomous being ... so she freely goes to the sea, losing her life. But she does not lose her self."[12]

By beginning and ending *The Awakening* with the sea Chopin gives the book a wholeness that Edna cannot find in her life. Furthermore, Chopin's themes of sea/mother, love/lover, self/birth, sexuality/creativity are joined as Edna's birth of a new self is juxtaposed against Adèle's giving birth to another. In a moment of liberty she stands naked on the beach feeling like "some new-born creature" before entering the sea which becomes the universal Great Mother. To be sure, Chopin uses one image of defeat, the "bird with the broken wing," which Edna sees "reeling, fluttering, circling, disabled down down to the water." (124) This was the image used by Mlle. Reisz when, as if predicting Edna's fall she said, "it is a sad spectacle to see the weakling bruised, exhausted, fluttering back to earth." (89) But how strong must a woman be at this time in order to maintain her artistic vocation without any support from community? Certainly Mlle. Reisz has given Edna no encouragement, so Edna thinks of how she would have laughed at her, of Robert who would never understand, and of her children who "sought to drag her into the soul's slavery." (123)

Yet Edna's final moment is one of autonomous sexuality, as the world of her imagination resonates with fertility — "There was the hum of bees, and the musky odor of pinks filled the air." (125) Chopin repeats the description of the sea which describes Edna's first swim, "The touch of the sea is sensuous, enfolding the body in its soft, close embrace," (124) and with this symbolic closure portrays Edna becoming whole in the only way she can, by immersion in the universal sea of love. But how can Edna's death be positive? Many critics think it is not.[13] Wolff, for example, uses it as further evidence of Edna's regressive instincts.[14] Christ believes that while the ending of the novel was realistic for its time, suicide as a resolution cannot satisfy women now.[15] Nevertheless, Edna Pontellier succeeds in giving birth to a new self even though the fact that she can not live on earth as this new self is tragic. The triumph of *The Awakening* lies in Chopin's depicting, when others did not, the conflicts faced by women who wish to become artists. Courageously, she built in her novel a bridge from past to future so that women might find their way across. Like her heroine, she too was a *pontellier*, a bridgemaker.

Notes

1. C.L. Deyo, "The Newest Books," St. Louis *Post-Dispatch*, May 20, 1899, quoted in Kate Chopin, *The Awakening*, an authoritative text, Context, Criticisms (New York, Norton, 1976), p. 149.

2. Kate Chopin, *The Awakening & Selected Stories of Kate Chopin* (New York: The New American Library, 1976), p. 120. All quotes are cited from this edition,
3. Cynthia Griffin Wolff, "Thanatos and Eros: Kate Chopin's *The Awakening*," *American Quarterly* XXV (Oct. 1973), printed in *The Awakening*, ed. Culley, p. 212, 217.
4. Suzanne Wolkenfeld, "Edna's Suicide: The Problem of the One and the Many," in *The Awakening* ed. Culley, p. 223.
5. James Justus, "The Unawakening of Edna Pontellier." *Southern Literary Journal,* X (Spring, 1978), p. 112.
6. Donald A. Ringe, "Romantic Imagery in Kate Chopin's *The Awakening*," *American Literature*, 43 (January, 1972), reprinted in *The Awakening*, ed. Culley, p. 206.
7. Carol. P. Christ, *Diving Deep and Surfacing: Women Writers on Spiritual Quest* (Boston: Beacon Press, 1980), p. 35.
8. Per Seyersted, *Kate Chopin: A Critical Biography* (Baton Rouge: Louisiana State University Press, 1969), p. 153.
9. Sandra Gilbert and Susan Gubar, *The Madwoman in the Attic: The Woman Writer and the Nineteenth Century Literary Imagination* (New Haven: Yale University Press, 1979), p. 50.
10. Sylvia Plath, *The Bell Jar* (New York: Harper & Row, 1971), p. 53.
11. Plath, p. 53.
12. Anne Goodwyn Jones, *Tomorrow Is Another Day: The Women Writer in the South, 1859-1936* (Baton Rouge: Louisiana State University Press, 1981), p. 169.
13. Wolkenfeld sums up critical views of Edna's suicide in *The Awakening*, ed. Culley. Those cited who hold negative views are Donald S. Rankin, George M. Spangler, and Cynthia Griffin Wolff.
14. Wolff, in *The Awakening*, ed. Culley, p. 218.
15. Christ, p. 39.

Gertrude Stein: The pattern moves, the woman behind shakes it

LINDA MIZEJEWSKI

Mellon Foundation, University of Kentucky

SINCE GERTRUDE STEIN's *Tender Buttons* was published in 1914, its colorful chunks of language and imagery have been shaken in the kaleidoscopes of a dozen critical modes to produce a myriad of readings, designs, and explanations. The multitude of critical approaches attests to its brilliance and obscurity at once: readers presented with this wild, semi-verbless appraisal of objects, food, and rooms are justifiably intimidated but also challenged to find the "key" to a work in which "A Piece of Coffee" is "More of a double. A place in no new table," and in which "Red Roses" are "Cool red rose and a pink cut pink, a collapse and a sold hole, a little less hot."[1]

Tender Buttons has been described as a series of prose poems, although no traditional genre can do justice to its departures from all traditions, genres, and syntax. Divided into three sections, "Objects," "Food," and "Rooms," it uses things, occasions, or phrases as the starting points of "descriptions" that do not describe or "definitions" that do not define. Under "Objects" we find word-portraits or meditations on everything from the trivial to the obscure: "A Substance in a Cushion," "Dirt and Not Copper," "A Shawl," "It Was Black, Black Took." "Food" begins with a sensual five-page contemplation of "Roast Beef" ("There is coagulation in cold and there is none in prudence. Something is preserved and the evening is long and the colder spring has sudden shadows in a sun," p. 481) and

Women's Studies, 1986
Vol. 13, pp. 033-047
0049-7878/86/1302-0033 $18.50/0

moves on to "Sugar," "Lunch," "Orange In," and so on. "Rooms" is the last and longest piece, describing space as tangentially as any of the previous pieces had "described," and including non-linear, semi-syntactical observations that are alternately rhapsodical and comic: "Alike and a snail, this means Chinamen, it does there is no doubt that to be right is more than perfect there is no doubt and glass is confusing it confuses the substance which was of a color. . . . Startling a starved husband is not disagreeable" (p.500). As several critics have pointed out, the text is meant to be read aloud and its sense of humor cannot be ignored in the most serious of its readings.

These various readings, and the causes to which *Tender Buttons* has been rallied, include automatic writing, literary Cubism, religious mysticism, linguistic experimentation, perceptual innovation, Jungian "mandala," post-modernist narrative, and conflict with Stein's brother Leo. Without denying the validity of these readings — and crediting the genius of the text for accomodating multiple readings — I would like to propose one more, one that illuminates a relationship between Stein and several women modernist writers. The third party in this nexus is Alfred North Whitehead, whose thinking has been linked to Stein in the past and who was named by Stein, along with herself and Picasso, as one of the three "first class geniuses" of her lifetime.[2] For the past decade, feminist philosophers have aligned themselves with Whitehead's process thought as a viable metaphysics for a feminist perspective. Taking this idea into the literary realm, a Whiteheadian perspective clarifies the dilemma of self-identification that occurs in the works of several feminist modernists: Virginia Woolf, Charlotte Perkins Gilman, Katherine Mansfield, and Kate Chopin. By identifying the similarities in Stein's and Whitehead's idea of self, we can understand the problem posed frequently in modernist literature, that of the integrated self caught in the language and philosophy of a dualistic culture.

Such a reading is not a "standard" feminist reading of Stein, as for example Cynthia Secor would give us in her biographical approach to Stein's novel *Ida*. Secor sees Stein's womanhood and lesbianism as the dynamic of her work: a radical re-definition of self and reality in reaction to patriarchal culture. Secor's thesis concentrates on *Ida*, but she refers to *Tender Buttons* briefly as a "celebration of the domestic and sensual aspects of [Stein's] relation with Toklas."[3]

Such a reading, I believe, tends to attach a literalness of narrative to the text which seems to strain too much in the direction of "meaning." As Pamela Hadas notes, "It is interesting, in a way, to go through *Tender Buttons* as one would a book of riddles trying to guess the 'answers' ... but this approach (as [Stein] surely knew and was amused by) can only lead to overingenuousness on the one hand and frustration on the other."[4] Seeing life with Alice as the "answer to the riddle" cheats *Tender Buttons* of its linguistic and perceptual answer-in-itself described by Bridgeman, Hoffman, and Weinstein.

My approach to Stein is, on the other hand, feminist in an indirect way. I am connecting Stein with other female modernists through a consciousness that I believe can be accurately described as White-headian. While Secor believes that Stein is reacting *primarily* to patriarchal culture as a woman, I am asserting that she is reacting *primarily* to a problem in language and self-perception that is part of the accoutrement of that patriarchal culture, a problem for men and women alike, but which manifests itself in the writing of women in a particular way. My purpose is not to claim *Tender Buttons* as a feminist text, but to show how Stein might be a link to a Whiteheadian consciousness that is as useful for feminist readers and writers as it has been for feminist philosophers.

The dilemma of self-identification in modernism arises in a tension between delineation and flux, between the need for a room of one's own and the resistance to confinement. Woolf's Mrs. Dalloway, for example, is suspended in this kind of self-perception: "She sliced like a knife through everything; at the same time was outside, looking on."[5] This tension strains between the yearning for knife-like integrity and the knowledge that the self is not a "knife" at all, but a fluid process sunk into multiple processes. This sensibility is complicated in that the values of autonomy and affinity are set into opposition in our culture and related to gender. Valerie C. Saiving, describing traditional modes of identity, uses the terms "individuality" and "related-ness" to describe sexual stereotypes:

We are taught that men are ... *essentially* self-directing, autonomous, and unique individuals whose needs, interests, and activities are valuable in themselves. In

contrast, we learn ... that women are, or should strive to become, beings whose existence is *essentially* constituted by their relationships to others.[6]

In such a dichotomy, the woman naming the self as separate is considered unnatural; moreover, her definitions and names are those
imposed by a male culture, as Mary Daly and others have pointed
out.[7]

Resistance to names and boundaries occurs in a number of women
writers and their protagonists in the early part of the century when the
confining definitions imposed by the Cult of True Womanhood were
being defied. Barbara Welter describes the demands of True Womanhood as "piety, purity, submissiveness, and domesticity. Put them all
together and they spelled mother, daughter, sister, wife — woman."[8]
When Stein wittily gives the non-definition of "Custard" as "Not to
be. Not to be narrowly" (p. 490), she could be giving the motto for Kate
Chopin's protagonist in *The Awakening*, for Woolf's undefinable
Orlando, or for several of the women in Katherine Mansfield's
stream-of-consciousness story "Prelude." The women in "Prelude,"
in fact, give us a paradigm of the dilemma: they are expected to fall into
patterns like the domestic ones they arrange: "Everything in the
kitchen had become part of a series of patterns" for the arranging
grandmother,[9] but her daughter, stultified in the male-defined roles of
child-bearer and mate, is happiest when she is left alone, when the
patterns of the walls themselves begin to move:

... she traced a poppy on the wallflower. ... In the quiet, and under her tracing finger,
the poppy seemed to come alive ... Things had a habit of coming alive like that. Not
only large substantial things like furniture, but curtains and the patterns of stuffs ...
(p. 68).

Driven much further into madness by her condescending husband
and her circumscribed Victorian life, the narrator of Charlotte Perkins
Gilman's "The Yellow Wallpaper" hallucinates the trapped woman
behind the wallpaper in her room: "The front pattern *does* move —
and no wonder!" she discovers excitedly, "The woman behind shakes
it!"[10] She has had a long history of having "to be narrowly."

Of all these protagonists, only Orlando, in the fantasy of easy androgyny, is not disturbed, repressed, or mad. Edna Pontellier of *The Awakening* does not survive her journey into selfhood at all; she clearly knows what she does *not* want to be, but in rejecting one set of structures — the True Womanhood precepts — she finds herself in another: the structures and patterns of heterosexual romance.[11] Disappointed in the latter, she feels she has no choices, no delineated self. Only the water seems unstructured enough; swimming is her way of "reaching out for the unlimited in which to lose herself."[12] Her "unlimited" sense of self, however, can be attained only by her self-extinction. Likewise, Gilman's narrator of "The Yellow Wallpaper" pulls herself out of the patterns at the price of her sanity. Finally, the women of "Prelude" float like ghosts in their male world, feeling unconnected to their private "real" selves. The young unmarried Beryl is miserable, sensing that her trained flirtatiousness and defence to men is a "false" self. "She saw the real Beryl — a shadow ... A shadow. Faint and unsubstantial she shone. What was there of her except the radiance? And for what tiny moments she was really she" (p. 98). The "unsubstantial" self has no mode of being. Like the other women in the house, she ends by dressing and answering for and to men, complying with her society's given definitions because the undefined self remains elusive and inarticulate.

In all cases, the non-delineated self, in a culture that respects clear-cut, autonomous classifications, has no power. Woolf's woman writer, after all, needs a room of her own not simply for practical purposes, but for the self-definition, the self-assertion of having private space. Mrs. Dalloway's habitual retreat to her attic room is a deliberate refusal of her role as wife/mother and an assertion of an earlier, purer self:

So the room was an attic; the bed narrow; and lying there reading, for she slept badly, she could not dispel a virginity preserved through childbirth which clung to her like a sheet. Lovely in girlhood, suddenly there came a moment ... when, through some contraction of this cold spirit, she had failed [her husband] (p. 46).

The ambiguous nature of the retreat, however, is revealed in the connotations of death, the retreat from life itself: the narrow bed is a coffin as well as a virginal renewal; the sheet a shroud. The "cold spirit" in its refusal of sexuality is also a refusal of life.

Moreoever, Mrs. Dalloway is later confused when her life-expanding empathy, which seems to dissolve walls and rooms, is confronted by the terrible facts of the rooms themselves. She watches the old woman in the next house move as Big Ben strikes, and senses that the woman moves "as if she were attached to that sound, that string. Gigantic as it was, it had something to do with her . . . Clarissa tried to follow her . . ." (pp. 192-3). Unfortunately, her sense of being connected to the woman, having "something to do with her" like the sound, is elusive, is both true and not: "And the supreme mystery . . . was simply this: here was one room; there another" (p. 193). The self remains in the confines of its walls, retreats to it, and at the same time resists those walls.

Stein's *Tender Buttons* resembles, in its methods, this wall-dissolving, pattern-shaking motif. Without ascribing to it a theme or narrative, we can at least see in it a consciousness that is deliberately breaking down categories of perception, time, space, and language. Rebelling against the confinements of definition, Stein liberates our habitual ways of seeing ordinary objects. She turns our eye to what the domestic woman traditionally deals with: household objects, kitchen items, the home. Then she explodes our traditional perceptions, asking us to understand eye-glasses as "A color in shaving" (p. 470), or asparagus as "wet wet weather" (p. 491). Her own categorization into "Objects," "Food," and "Rooms" is deliberately deceptive, for her definitions overlap, the distinctions break down, so that "Roast Beef" sounds like a room, "In the inside there is sleeping, in the outside there is reddening" (p. 477), while a room is described as time and action: "The author of all that is in there behind the door and that is entering in the morning. Explaining darkening and expecting relating is all of a piece" (p. 499). Sometimes the object is a series of impressions: "A Petticoat" is "A white light, a disgrace, an ink spot, a rosy charm" (p. 471). At other times the object is a process: "Milk" is "Climb up in sight climb up in the whole utter needles and a guess a whole guess is hanging" (p. 487). The total effect is a radical shaking of the categorical Victorian world.

Given the linguistic eccentricities of this text, it is not difficult to see why early critics wrote it off as an experiment in "automatic writing," a phenomenon Stein had researched in medical school.[13] Later critics related it to the techniques of Picasso, explaining that Stein's refractions of reality are the literary equivalent of Cubism. Michael Hoffman, who once allied himself with that theory, later qualified, explaining that the use of one medium to describe another is "at best a metaphor." Stein's association with Picasso is not entirely irrelevant, however, for as Hoffman points out, "What she opted for was the same freedom to dislocate the previous forms and concentrations of the literary tradition."[14] Most critics have concurred in that opinion, and detailed analyses of the poetic and stylistic techniques have begun with the assumption that Stein's purpose is the achievement of a new mode of perception, one that begins with the object but does not remain with it, and one that constructs the moment in an alternate perception of time.[15] Stein herself calls this structure of time "the continuous present," which she says is "a natural composition in the world . . . I knew nothing of a continuous present but it came naturally to me to make one."[16]

Of *Tender Buttons* Stein wrote, "I struggled with the ridding of myself of nouns."[17] She does not quite succeed in doing that, only occasionally discarding syntax altogether: "Aider, why aider why whow whow stop touch" is her description of the last "object" in the first section — actually not an object at all but the statement, "This Is the Dress, Aider" (p. 476). Even an impressionistic "More" depends on nouns: "An elegant use of foliage and grace and a little piece of white cloth and oil" (p. 469). Studies of her language are as numerous as studies of her perceptual experimentation. Norman Weinstein explains the syntactical play as an approximation of the attempt of consciousness to articulate experience as it occurs. He calls the gathering of the chaotic multitude of words "the linguistic moment."[18] Like other critics, Weinstein is interested in Stein's part in the creation of a modernist literature that takes linguistic risks in order more accurately to catch human perception. Critic Neil Schmitz goes further than this, however, seeing in *Tender Buttons* a heralding of the "post-modernist" concerns with narrative and point of view taken up later by Barthes and Barthelme.[19] Stein looms in the venerable position, then, of one of the recognized architects of modern literature, and *Tender Buttons* as its monument. Weinstein calls the work "a child's first guide to the twentieth century" (Weinstein, p. 67), though it is, ironically, considered unreadable by a majority of twentieth-century readers.

The relationship of Stein's alternate modes of perception to the philosophy of Alfred North Whitehead has been frequently cited and accurately qualified by critics who point out that the iconoclastic Stein is no philosopher.[20] Allegra Stewart, however, connects the theory of religion and art shared by Stein and Whitehead, the creative act and the act of meditation, both being acts of "presence, by which the dualism of experience is overcome here and now ... Knower and known are joined ...".[21] Reading *Tender Buttons* as an act of meditation, Stewart makes the point that it is an attempt to unify the dissociations of experience. She later takes this further in an extended Jungian interpretation of Stein, in which *Tender Buttons* is seen as a "mandala," a ritualistic meditative prayer structured to bring the subconscious in contact with the universal subconscious.[22] In general, this, along with Secor's feminist interpretation, is one of the few readings that attempts to see *Tender Buttons* as other than a linguistic, narrative, and perceptual experiment.[23]

With Bridgman, Hoffman, and Weinstein, I agree that interest in the text must center on its method, not its meaning, and that its method is directly concerned with the presentation of an alternate means of perception. While such critics do justice to the *art* of Stein's dealing with the "continuous present," however, I feel the need to extend this approach into its philosophical implications. Placing Stein into the context of Whiteheadian process thought does not tailor her into a philosopher, for she resisted systematic philosophies as much as she resisted categories of identity. Process thought, however, gives us a way of understanding not only a work such as *Tender Buttons*, but the sensibility of a Mrs. Dalloway, an Edna Pontellier, and a Mrs. Ramsay. If feminist philosophers are right, such an understanding might help us in the shifting of attitudes necessary to achieve an androgynous culture.

Such a reading requires that Whiteheadian thought be considered seriously, not just in its general ideas about religion or creativity, but in its metaphysics. While a comprehensive analysis is not possible in this format, a brief summary is necessary. Whiteheadian metaphysics differs from most philosophical systems in that the latter ask us to think of ourselves as rooms in which events (thoughts, experience) occur, while Whitehead asks us to think of ourselves as events, constantly coming into being through interaction which other events — which include perceptions, actions, other persons, and the immediate and distant past. These multiple "pulsations" of process unite in "concrescence" to constitute a moment of experience. The individual person's "subjective aim" is capable of infinite creativity in the use of past and present moments of process, and the person is in fact made up of a complexity of past and present occasions, always in the moment of creation.[24]

Stein's method of the "continuous present" is congruent with Whitehead's description of how the present moment actually occurs and how the individual consciousness "occurs" *with* the present moment. It is certainly easier to think of the items in *Tender Buttons* as "occurrences" rather than "descriptions." The "experience" of the object is occurring simultaneously with a multitude of other physical and mental experiences — or prehensions. The radical subjectivity of the text, then, prevents an "analysis" not only of the New Critical variety, but of the feminist literary variety, too, for such readings ultimately depend on meaning and relationship to at least a minimally objective reality. On the other hand, philosophical analysis is equally unsuitable as the final "key" to this work. We can only say that Whiteheadian process thought gives us a way to approach it by placing it into a context that Stein would have approved — sanctifying Whitehead's view of reality by enshrining him in that sacred trio with herself and Picasso.

Whitehead is especially concerned about the "mistaken" perception of reality and individuals as "enduring substances." "The simple notion of an enduring substance sustaining persistent qualities ... expresses a useful abstract for many purposes of life," he writes. "But whenever we try to use it as a fundamental statement of the nature of things, it proves itself mistaken."[25] In *Tender Buttons*, no object, space, or person "endures" in time. "A Brown," for example, is "Not liquid not more so is relaxed and yet there is a change, a news is pressing" (p. 473). In "Rooms" she explains changes in space in this way: "Explaining darkening and expecting relating is all of a piece ... and yet there comes a change, there comes the time to press more air. This does not mean the same as disappearance" (p. 499). The "change" is clearly not an "event" in the conventional understanding, nor is the color a "thing," nor is the person a delineated entity: "A Little Called Pauline" is "A little called anything shows shudders. Come and say what prints all day. A whole few watermelon. There is no pope" (p. 473). We can call this "stream of consciousness," or "the linguistic moment," or "free association," but as a "description" of Pauline it certainly opposes our traditional idea of personhood. The notion of enduring substances, says Whitehead, "arose from a mistake and has never succeeded in any of its applications. But is has had one success: *it has entrenched itself in language*, in Aristotelian logic, and in metaphysics" (italics mine).[26]

The "entrenchment" in language Whitehead refers to here has to do with constructions of Aryan languages which separate person from action. Such a language is fairly incapable of expressing a Whiteheadian (and Steinian) perception of reality — though one might argue that the visual arts are more capable of doing so in phenomena such as Cubism. When Stein tells us that she is attempting to "rid" herself of nouns, she is imagining a process language — one entirely made of verbs — that Whitehead must have admired when he met her a few years later in the "beautiful country" around Paris: "Doctor Whitehead and Gertrude Stein never ceased wandering around in it and talking about all things."[27]

Relating Stein's breakdown of language to the breaking down of the categorical modes of perception and identification, critics such as Weinstein have readily connected her to major trends in modernism. If we further link her perspective to a Whiteheadian one, then the sensibility of the modernist writers discussed previously can also be examined in the perspective of process thought. In Woolf, Gilman, Mansfield, and Chopin, characters who vacillate between defined identity and the flux of interrelatedness fear that the latter will result in a loss of "self."[28] Mrs. Dalloway, Edna Pontellier, and the "Prelude" women retreat to rooms and enclosed spaces because they sense that their only means of self-assertion consists in claiming such defined spaces.[29] This retreat is, in fact, the metaphor culture has given them: the self as an "enduring substance" in space, asserted by ownership of space — colonization, conquests of frontiers, capitalism. In such a culture, too, Edna Pontellier's search for self in *The Awakening* instinctively takes her out of her husband's home and into her own "pigeon-house." The move to different space fails, however, and she later understands all her options as pigeonholes too narrow and bound for her liking.

When these protagonists feel they have no options, they are expressing the reality of their language and cultural perception, which divided "self" and "other" categorically and absolutely.[30] In Whiteheadian metaphysics, on the other hand, such a dichotomy is impossible, for the "self" is *constituted* of its interrelations with all other experience. Saiving explains that in process thought, "Not only are individuality and relatedness compatable aspects of every actuality, these two principles require each other. And since they require each other, neither is more 'real,' important, or valuable than the other."[31]

Consequently, the experience of these protagonists as *both* self and other is a more "true" experience than that of the autonomous self. There is no doubt that the "truth" Gilman's tormented narrator of "The Yellow Wallpaper" sees in the shifting wall patterns is more valid than the sane, honeyed, artificial world imposed upon her by her husband: "'Bless her little heart!' said he with a big hug 'she shall be as sick as she pleases! But now let's improve the shining hours by going to sleep ...'" (Gilman, p. 24). Likewise, Edna Pontellier, shaking all the patterns of her previous life, is condescendingly humored by her husband, to whom her new behavior is either sick or mad. Edna's "problem" is her refusal to identify with a single, recognizable "self;" when she "searches" for a new identity, she expects actually to *find* one — unable to understand that her self *is* the process of its changes. Again, the villain is cultural expectation of enduring consciousness. Cartesian philosophy, Whitehead points out, "conceives the thinker as creating the occasional thought. The philosophy of organism inverts the order, and conceives the thought as a constituent in the creation of the occasional thinker."[32]

Is this tension between "self" and "interrelatedness" an intrinsically female problem? Saiver has pointed out that women are traditionally expected to be more "related" to others than men. Penelope Washbourn, writing of the female experience and its expression in process thought, notes that the experience of pregnancy and menstrual cycles tend to "erode" in women traditional distinctions between self/other and mind/body.[33] Certainly the dilemmas of the previously discussed protagonists are centered on female sexual experience — on wifehood and motherhood. The sexual experience, then, may trigger the self/other or substance/flux problem in women in a particular way because sexuality more obviously demonstrates to women the metaphysics that Whitehead claims is actually universal. However, the problem is a cultural one, not an inherently female one, and further study would show, I think, that the problem manifests itself in the writings of men in other ways.

Having placed Stein's *Tender Buttons* in these contexts, I believe that this approach accords with that of Anna Gibbs, who uses the feminist criticism of French novelist Hélène Cixous to understand Stein "in terms of the possibilities she opens up for other women writers."[34] Gibbs too avoids a biographical-feminist reading of Stein and allies herself and Cixous with a "third wave" of feminist criticism that centers on writing as self-creation and self-naming. She finds that Stein and Cixous share the dynamics of transformation and repetition that produce "entity writing" instead of "identity writing." Entity writing concentrates on continuous presence, "so that consciousness is forced to become reflexive, and writing becomes a process of concentration, or intensification" (p. 288).

This concept of writing as "intensification," which is repetitious in its exploring of the alternate possibilities of the moment, is very similar to Whitehead's description of the creative process in *Religion in the Making*. While all existence is naturally "creating" in process, the artist "brings together something which is actual and something which, at its entry into the process, is not actual."[35] The novelty must *resemble* the actual, "but it must contrast with it in respect to contrary instances so as to obtain vividness and quality" (p. 115). Donald W. Sherburne has done an extended study of Whiteheadian aesthetics and explains the metaphysics of creativity as a "horizontal" prehension of experience, which is usually prehended "vertically." The creative perception is sensitive to areas of consciousness not explored in commonplace experience; while "vertical" perception involves the integration of microcosmic entities into one macrocosmic prehension, the "horizontal" and creative perception is able to "concentrate macrocosmic entities into *one focal point of experience*."[36]

Thinking of *Tender Buttons* in relation to Whitehead is, I hope, a "horizontal" perception of several modernist writers and ideas. It involves the belief that feminist criticism must look beyond social context in literature to the philosophical context as a way to pinpoint the dilemmas of self-identity. The result may give us a more "complete" perspective on our experience in the world. Whitehead gives us a complex but viable model for that perspective, while Stein, ultimately iconoclastic, gives us the sound and sense of it: "The care with which there is incredible justice and likeness," she concludes, "all this makes a magnificent asparagus, and also a fountain" (p. 450).

Notes

1. Gertrude Stein, *Tender Buttons*, in *Selected Writings of Gertrude Stein*, ed. Carl Van Vechten (New York: Modern Library, 1945), pp. 463 and 472. All references to the text come from this edition.
2. Gertrude Stein, *The Autobiography of Alice B. Toklas*, in *Selected Writings of Gertrude Stein*, p. 5.
3. Cynthia Secor, "*Ida*, A Great American novel," *Twentieth Century Literature*, 24 (1978), 100.
4. Pamela Hadas, "Spreading the Difference: One Way to Read Gertrude Stein's *Tender Buttons*," *Twentieth Century Literature*, 24 (1978), 64.
5. Virginia Woolf, *Mrs Dalloway* (New York: Harcourt Brace, 1925), p. 11.
6. Valerie C. Saiving, "Androgynous Life: A Feminist Appropriation of Process Thought," in *Feminism and Process Thought: Harvard Divinity School/Claremont Christian Center for Process*, ed. Sheila Davaney (Lewiston, N.Y.: Edwin Mellen Press, 1981), pp. 18-19.
7. Mary Daly, *Beyond God the Father: Toward a Philosophy of Women's Liberation* (Boston: Beacon, 1973), p. 8.
8. Barbara Welter, "The Cult of True Womanhood," *American Quarterly*, 28 (1966), 152.
9. Katherine Mansfield, "Prelude," in *Stories* (New York: Random House, 1956), p. 70.
10. Charlotte Perkins Gilman, *The Yellow Wallpaper* (Boston, 1899; rpt. New York: Feminist Press, 1973), p. 30.
11. Jean Wyatt, "Thoughts on Fantasy in *The Awakening*," N.E.H. Seminar, U. of Cal., Davis, 1981.
12. Kate Chopin, *The Awakening* (1899; rpt. New York: Avon, 1972), p. 48.
13. B.F. Skinner, "Has Gertrude Stein a Secret?" *Atlantic*, Jan., 1934, pp. 53-57.
14. Michael J. Hoffman, Gertrude Stein (Boston: Twayne, 1976), p. 59.
15. See Robert Bridgman, *Gertrude Stein in Pieces* (New York: Oxford 1970) and Michael J. Hoffman, *The Development of Abstractionism in the Work of Gertrude Stein*

(Philadelphia: U. of Pa. Press, 1965), pp. 175-95.

16. Gertrude Stein, "Composition as Explanation," in *Selected Writings of Gertrude Stein*, p. 517.

17. Gertrude Stein, *Lectures in America*, quoted in Van Vechten's introduction to *Tender Buttons* in Selected Writings, p. 460.

18. Norman Weinstein, *Gertrude Stein and the Literature of Modern Consciousness* (New York: Frederick Ungar, 1970), p. 62.

19. Neil Schmitz, "Gertrude Stein as Post-Modernist: The Rhetoric of *Tender Buttons*," *Journal of Modern Literature*, 3 (1974), 1208-18.

20. Rosalind S. Miller, *Gertrude Stein: Form and Intelligibility* (New York: Exposition Press, 1949), pp. 47-48; also see Weinstein, p. 57.

21. Allegra Stewart, "The Quality of Gertrude Stein's Creativity," *American Literature*, 28 (1957), 496.

22. Allegra Stewart, *Gertrude Stein and the Present* (Cambridge: Harvard, 1967), p. 72.

23. See Pamela Hadas' work, which sees *Tender Buttons* as an articulation of the tensions between Stein and her brother Leo in the transition time when Alice Toklas had come into Stein's life and her brother was about to leave it.

24. See Alfred North Whitehead, *Process and Reality: An Essay in Cosmology*, corrected ed., eds. David Ray Griffin and Donald W. Sherburne (New York: Macmillan, 1929; rpt. 1978). For the beginning reader of Whitehead, an easier summary is provided in the Saiving article.

25. Whitehead, p. 79.

26. *Ibid.*

27. Gertrude Stein, *The Autobiography*, p. 145.

28. Anna S. Benajmin has done a thorough and brilliant analysis of the structure and "view of reality" in *Mrs. Dalloway* using a Whiteheadian approach in "Towards an Understanding of Virginia's Woolf's *Mrs. Dalloway*," *Wisconsin Studies in Contemporary Literature*, 6 (1965), 214-227. While Benjamin emphasizes the structure of reality in the novel, I would press it further to show a problem of identity in Clarissa Dalloway that can be understood with process thought.

29. Another interesting point of view on rooms is given in James Naremore's *The World Without a Self: Virginia Woolf and the Novel* (New Haven and London: Yale, 1973), pp. 240-44.

30. It is interesting to speculate if our culture's dichotomy of perception is responsible for the development of schizophrenia. Maremore, discussing Virginia Woolf's expression of reality, brings up R. D. Laing's descriptions of a certain schizophrenic symptom of feeling a rush of "oneness" with the world followed by a rush of terror that the self will be "absorbed" wholly into this world and "lost." Naremore mentions this, he says, to illustrate that part of Woolf's psychosis may have been incorporated into her lucid creativity (Naremore, p. 247). Nevertheless, we can wonder if the "schizophrenic" feels terror only because he has been conditioned to think that the "dissolving" of the self into a "oneness" is a terrible thing.

31. Saiving, p. 26.

32. Whitehead, p. 267

33. Penelope Washbourne, "The Dynamics of Female Experience: Process Models and Human Values," in *Feminism and Process Thought*, pp. 93-94.

34. Anna Gibbs, "Helene Cixous and Gertrude Stein: New Directions in Feminist Criticism," *Meanjin Quarterly*, 38 (1979), p. 291.
35. Alfred North Whitehead, *Religion in the Making* (New York: Macmillan, 1926), p. 114.
36. Donald W. Sherburne, *A Whiteheadian Aesthetic* (New Haven: Yale, 1961), p. 162.

Wilfred Owen and Abram

CARYN McTIGHE MUSIL

English Department, La Salle University

A WEEK AFTER World War I broke out, Wilfred Owen wrote to his brother, "After all my years of playing soldiers, and then of reading history, I have almost a mania to be in the East, to see fighting, and to serve."[1] He resisted his "mania" for another sixteen months, but by January, 1917, he found himself a commissioned officer at the Front. At first his early enthusiasm for the war survived. "There is a fine heroic spirit about being in France,"[2] he wrote in early January and after hearing the guns for the first time reported, "It was a sound not without a certain sublimity."[3] Two days later he wrote home, "There is nothing in all this inferno but mud and thunder,"[4] and within ten days confessed, "We were wretched beyond my previous imagination."[5] Out of such wretchedness some of the greatest anti-war poetry in the English language was written. As Owen came to repudiate the war, he bitterly condemned with all the ferocity of a son's disillusionment the fathers who were orchestrating the meticulous slaughter. Like other modernists, Owen was not merely railing against the carnage he witnessed; he was, finally, profoundly opposed to the patriarchal culture that seemed to make war such an inevitability and the stubborn continuation of it so imperative.

The values of this culture were carefully inscribed by a powerful male tradition in texts that taught young boys how to become men. These tablets contained inherited masculine wisdom about how to perpetuate a world where male political and sexual dominance would continue. In a letter to Siegfried Sassoon on October 10, 1918, Owen writes, less than a month before he was killed at the Front, "One day I will write Deceased over many books."[6] His assaults on those male-

Women's Studies, 1986
Vol. 13, pp. 049-061
0049-7878/86/1302-0049 $18.50/0

authored books permeate the letters and poetry of the posthumously decorated warrior. To subvert his male legacy, Owen provides us with a text of his own in which he tells the truth about what it means to be a man. "The true Poets must be truthful," he says in his Preface. In speaking truth, Owen violates the secret conspiracy between fathers and sons to remain silent about failure, inadequacy, or disagreement. Despite Freudian theories, there is no reconciliation with the father, at least not for Owen. The son does not eventually assume his throne in the patriarch's kingdom. Instead Owen rejects the king and kingdom outright.

While fathers have sent their sons to die in other wars, the casualties of World War I were so staggering that the usual generational cycles were shattered. Six months fighting around Verdun in 1916 surpassed the total casualties of 400,000 from America's four-year Civil War, and on the Somme in five months alone there were more than one million casualties. By the end of the War the average age of the soldiers was under nineteen and the minimum height requirement had been dropped to 5′4″. Owen was constantly assaulted by visual evidence of fathers literally sending boys to die. Rather than be silently sacrificed to his father's sentence, Owen uses his voice to challenge the authority and veracity of inherited notions from his father's culture of nationalism, masculinity, and sexuality. Trying to sever his traditional loyalties, he seeks an alternative model of manhood by embracing forbidden female qualities in himself.

Reflecting his re-defined role as an outsider who disdains his father's lineage, Owen assumes a poetic identity with the prophets, outcasts from existing social orders who speak truths to an unreceptive populace. "All a poet can do today is warn," Owen claims in his Preface. Like all prophets, Owen warns primarily by telling the truth despite the fact that World War I was the most heavily censored war in history.[7] The most dangerous and subversive truth Owen tells is that fathers are murdering their sons, and doing so consciously. Many critics, from Lane to Stallworthy to Fussell, have commented on how Owen deliberately refers to soldiers as "boys," "youths," and "lads" to reinforce the sense of their innocence as they are subjected to war's obscene horrors. Such commentaries miss, however, Owen's implicit bitter attack against the father figure who is responsible, according to

Owen, for the death and mutilation of his own "boys." "The Parable of the Old Man and the Young" is Owen's most explicit poem about such inter-generational murder.

Using the Old Testament story of Abraham and Isaac as his literary analogue, Owen transformed the father, Abram, into the one who is willingly the military architect for his son's doom:

Then Abram bound the youth with belts and straps,
And builded parapets and trenches there,
And stretchèd forth the knife to slay his son.

The biblical story has an angel intervene to save Isaac at the last moment since Abraham has proven his willingness to obey God's orders. When a similar angel appears in Owen's poem, however, the scenario is radically different:

When lo! an angel called him out of heaven,
Saying, Lay not thy hand upon the lad,
Neither do anything to him. Behold,
A ram, caught in a thicket by its horns;
Offer the Ram of Pride instead of him.
But the old man would not so, but slew his son,
And half the seed of Europe, one by one.[8]

The patriarch Abram, like the patriarchs in power during Owen's life, breaks the covenant, ignores the divine voice, and establishes instead *his* male supremacy, his own version of the truth. In so doing, he creates the ritual that demands the endless yet meticulous slaughter of innocent male lambs rather than the single and redeeming sacrifice of the matured, arrogant male ego, "the Ram of Pride." Like Sir Douglas Haig, Commander-in-Chief of the British Forces, and Lloyd George, Prime Minister, the father stubbornly refuses to deviate from his chosen course, opting rather to slay his son and all sons in order to guarantee his pride. He thus enshrines a male rite for authority that demands awful and fatal initiations for sons.

In describing patriarchs as the real enemy of civilization and of God's kingdom, Owen, like D.H. Lawrence, offers a critique of the patriarchal institutions that had dominated western culture. By revealing murderous manipulations, Owen joins with other modernists who understood part of the social dynamics of the early twentieth century as hinging on the ferocious battle of the fathers against the sons. Owen appropriately uses Christian analogues to describe that bitter antagonism. In "The Parable" Isaac is described as a "lamb" and therefore is linked with Christ, another son who feels betrayed by his father and murdered that his father might have greater glory. That same struggle for dominion with the same defeat of the son occurs tellingly in "Soldier's Dream." There, too, Jesus, the peacemaker, is seen in opposition to his Father, the god of war.

I dreamed kind Jesus fouled the big-gun gears;
And caused a permanent stoppage in all bolts;
And buckled with a smile Mausers and Colts;
And rusted every bayonet with His tears.

And there were no more bombs, of ours or Theirs,
. . .
But God was vexed, and gave all power to Michael;
And when I woke he'd seen to our repairs.

God the Father, vexed with his son's audacity in stopping the war, reasserts power by reassembling the machinery of war. General Abram reigns once more. In another poem, "Inspection," the Abram-Haig-Lloyd George-God the Father figure reappears literally as "Field Marshall God." Owen continues to describe in a religious paradigm the generational warfare he witnesses. What he has salvaged from his shattered faith is not his reverence for God the Father, but for God the Son.

In pitting himself against Abram and his legions, Owen subverts, among other things, Abram's sacred book of nationalism by writing the truth about war, not the father's fictions. The dramatic impact of much of Owen's poetry depends on the juxtaposition of public claims or abstractions about war with the concrete, lived experience of war. "They are troops who fade, not flowers/For poets' tearful fooling," he writes in "Insensibility." And the soldiers "Bent double" "Knock-kneed," cursing and "coughing like hags" or "beggars" hardly match the shining, erect, smiling Tommies of World War I posters. "*Dulce et Decorum Est*" most effectively undermines the heroic code of yet another male text whose origins go back as far as Horace, claiming, "It is sweet and honorable to die for one's country." By forcing the reader to witness in minute, concrete detail just one soldier's gruesome death, the soldier persona in the poem shatters easy nationalistic slogans that lure innocent boys to war.

In a less well-known but still compelling poem, "Smile, Smile, Smile," Owen similarly undermines the patriarchs' banner of nationalism. The setting of the poem is a hospital for "half-limbed," "sunk-eyed wounded" veterans who are reading yet another text in the *Mail.* They are smiling ironically as they read the paper's lies and see exposed their fathers' motivations:

The sons we offered might regret they died
If we got nothing lasting in their stead.
We must be solidly indemnified.

Just as the above lines suggest the attention is on reimbursing and protecting the safe instigators of war rather than the unsafe enactors of war, so the following lines point to a similar obsession with self-interest clothed as nationalism:

We rulers sitting in this ancient spot
Would wrong our very selves if we forgot
The greatest glory will be theirs who fought,
Who kept this nation in integrity.

But where is the nation? And what is the attitude toward it of soldiers whose bodies were mutilated on its behalf? We are told they "smiled at one another curiously/Like secret men who knew their secret safe." The secret is that the "nation" resides *in* the sons themselves whom the "rulers" in their "ancient spot" have forfeited long ago:

(This is the thing they know and never speak,
That England one by one had fled to France,
Not many elsewhere now, save under France.)

Although the wounded soldiers keep their silence, their companion soldier Owen breaks it when he writes this poem. In attacking the manipulative use of nationalism as an excuse for continuing war, Owen speaks for the silent soldiers for the last time. It seems from all records to be the last poem Owen ever wrote.

Another script of the patriarchs which Owen subverts in addition to nationalism is the traditional definition of masculinity. In a number of poems he questions the socialization of young boys which seems to lead them inevitably to becoming soldiers. The officer in "A Terre" who is dying of wounds still says to his orderly:

Little I'd ever teach a son, but hitting,
Shooting, war, hunting, all the arts of hunting.
Well, that's what I learnt, — that, and making money.

The male tradition of sports also carried into the war the same skills and attitudes as those used on the playing fields. War was simply a more strenuous contest. So intertwined were the two male rituals of athletics and war that, as Paul Fussell has shown, in some assaults footballs were kicked towards enemy lines before an attack. The first recorded battle when a football was used this way was the Battle of Loos in 1915, a battle that produced 60,000 British casualties.[9]

Owen's response to such male socialization that makes sports, war, and life simply a contest of physical prowess and endurance is evident in one of his most moving poems, "Disabled." The veteran in this work, a boy not yet twenty, was a soccer player who internalized his culture's equation of sports and war:

One time he liked a blood-smear down his leg,
After the matches, carried shoulder-high.
It was after football, when he'd drunk a peg,
He thought he'd better join.

Less than a year after joining, he is sitting "in a wheeled chair, waiting for dark" "in his ghastly suit of grey,/Legless, sewn short at elbow." The women around him no longer cheer him on but "touch him like some queer disease."

For Owen, traditional notions of manhood included two important rites: initiation into the warrior myth and sexual initiation. The two intertwine and Owen refuses both. Though a warrior himself, Owen redefines what that really means. The young amputee veteran in "Disabled" originally imagined what being a warrior would be like through the language of other men like Tennyson or Morris or Kipling:

He thought of jewelled kilts
For daggers in plaid socks; of smart salutes;
And care of arms; and leave; and pay arrears.

"S.I.W." (Self-Inflicted Wound) dramatizes the suicidal imperative of the warrior myth for a young soldier who, filled with false rhetoric about male valor, shoots himself when the war deprives him of his own glorious death. The worst perpetrator of the myth in "S.I.W." significantly is the father.

Patting good-bye, doubtless they told the lad
He'd always show the Hun a brave man's face;
Father would sooner him dead than in disgrace, —
Was proud to see him going, aye, and glad.

"Death sooner than dishonour, that's the style!"
So Father said.

When the son, whose "Courage leaked, as sand/From the best sandbags after years of rain," finally plants the bullet in his own body which the enemy refused to, "It was the reasoned crisis of the soul." Indeed, the ethics of the father demanded the son's suicide.

One of Owen's better known peoms, "Arms and the Boy," continues his critique of the male warrior myth. It is a poem that describes the corruption of innocence in a boy seduced by weaponry. The alluring arms of war however, associate his maturation with the loss of Eden, "For his teeth seem for laughing round an apple." That the warrior myth is superimposed upon the youth's normal development is clear when we learn that he was not naturally equipped with weapons:

There lurk no claws behind his fingers supple;
And God will grow no talons at his heels,
Nor antlers through the thickness of his curls.

As the boy is transformed into a warrior, his mouth is filled with "cartridges of fine zinc teeth." The soldier fully armed is, in fact, transformed into the terrifyingly monstrous figure of the arms themselves: "Blue with all malice, like a madman's flash:/And thinly drawn with famishing for flesh."

In addition to rejecting fictions about the warrior myth, Owen rejects traditional male sexual initiation as well. In *The Great War and Modern Memory* Paul Fussell brilliantly describes Owen's homoerotic writing and places him in a larger cultural and literary tradition that extends from Whitman to Hopkins to Symond, all of whom celebrated the beauty and body of men or boys and honored the passionate bonds between them. Fussell uses the term homoerotic "to imply a sublimited (i.e. chaste) form of temporary homosexuality."[10] He argues that Owen's mind was "feeling always towards male particulars."[11] Consequently, his poetry is dominated by lads and boys and by parts of the body: mouths, limbs, hair, chest, hands. While it is true, as Fussell claims, that sexuality behind the lines provided a necessary counterbalance to carnage on the front, Owen's identification with the tradition of the homoerotic has at its roots a repudiation of the father's traditional heterosexuality.[12] The latter eventually comes to be linked in Owen's mind with the rape and violation of war, for Owen sees soldiers as the surrogate female rape victims.

Phallic symbols of the gun, especially in "Arms and the Boy" are described as frightening, vicious, seductive, and blood-thirsty. The sexual stimulation when the boy is lured "to stroke these blind, blunt bullet-leads" results in the boy's murder: the phallic bullets "long to nuzzle in the hearts of lads." The "arms" in the poem thus bring death not love. To avoid being a warrior/ravager, Owen rejects sexual initiation completely. A juvenile poem, "The Sleeping Beauty," has the prince kiss the sleeping princess, but without affect, presumably for either of them. He draws back since it was clearly "not my part,/To start voluptuous pulses in her heart." Owen continues to draw back from the role of the prince and in rejecting heterosexuality seems to reject practicing homosexuality as well. Though sensuous in his poetry, Owen remains above all chaste and in so doing claims identity with that chaste son, Jesus.

Assuming Christ's very words in "Greater Love," "Greater love hath no man than he lay down his life for his friends" (*John* 15:13), Owen posits a detailed rejection of male heterosexuality. What he rejects is the male creation through Petrarch and others of the appropriate female love object. He mocks Petrarchan red lips, luring eyes, slender body, soft gentle voice, full heart, and pale hands. All of these male designated female attributes are diminished next to the genuine love object — dying male soldiers. The new love object is, by contrast, curiously grotesque, violated, murdered. Still, it attracts Owen by its very victimization: "eyes blinded in my stead," "limbs knife-skewed/Rolling and rolling there," "cramp[ed] ... in death's extreme decrepitude," "hearts made great with shot." Owen echoes Christ's words at the end of the poem, this time on the cross when Jesus says, "Woman why weepest thou? ... Touch me not" (John 20:15-17). The woman in the poem may weep but the male sacrificed figure is now sanctified and beyond her reach. Thus Owen makes the greatest love of all that between men; woman may only watch and weep. In this poem Owen's very complicated sexual identity surfaces. He rejects father figures and heterosexuality, is drawn to traditional female qualities, yet clearly prefers men in arms to women's arms.

Raised in a world of boys' schools and surrounded only by men in the trenches, Owen has sensual antennae only for other men. Even in the early "Maundy Thursday," the persona reluctantly kneels at the altar to take the Eucharist. Instead of revering the Christ there who "was thin, and cold, and very dead," he kisses — even has his lips cling to — "the warm live hand" of the "server-lad." A later 1917 poem, "To My Friend," sustains a similar passion between two men. In it the persona is wondering what sort of monument he yearns for after death and prefers to be remembered only by his soldier's identity disk, one worn by his "sweet friend."

Inscribe no date nor deed
But may thy heart-beat kiss it, night and day,
Until the name grow blurred and fade away.

His sexual attraction for his friend is acknowledged but not acted on. The orgasm he would normally experience comes after his death as he fades away under his lover's kisses night and day.

More subversive of Abram's authority than his rejection of the warrior myth or male sexual initiations is Owen's acknowledgement and embrace of the "woman" in himself. While his locus is usually an exclusively male world, Owen recognizes the deadness and deathliness of traditional male legacies. Thus he turns to women's legacies for inspiration as he had turned to his own mother so often in his lifetime. Although Jon Stallworthy clearly prefers the sporting, gregarious Mr. Owen to the stoic, moral, and demanding Mrs. Owen, Owen himself did not share his biographer's preferences. Unabashedly his mother's favorite child, Owen was profoundly attached to his mother. His relation with his father was more distant. In his *Collected Letters*, for example, 554 of the 673 letters are addressed to his mother. Five are to his father. His salutations abound with "O most sweet among mothers" and he closes with phrases like "your Mother-languishing son." In one letter written from the Front, he confesses:

Without your Letters I should give in . . . without a definite object for carrying on. And that object is not my Motherland, which is a good land, nor my Mother tongue, which is a dear language, but for my Mother, of whom I am not worthy to be called
   the Son xxx[13]

His mother was the major influence in the poet's life, and according to Owen's brother Harold, responsible for his poetry:

It was in Broxton among the ferns and bracken and the little hills, secure in the safety and understanding love that my mother wrapped about him with such tender ministration, that the poetry in Wilfred, with gentle pushings, without hurt, began to bud, and not on the battlefields of France.[14]

In appropriating a matriarchal not a patriarchal tradition, Owen cultivates feelings, tenderness, and sensitivity. Most miraculous of all, he risks doing so in the most brutalizing and numbing of experiences. "My senses are charred," he writes, but insists, "I shall feel again as soon as I dare, but now I must not."[15] Owen's war experience also subjects him to situations that parallel many women's lives, especially in relationship to power and authority.[16] More powerful figures or forces typically impose self-division. In "The Snow," for example, the soldier in the poem is literally divided, first from the Earth and then from his body as Death shows him a worm and "the fresh-severed head of it, my head." Similarly in "Strange Meeting," set in a hellish underworld, the soldier meets an enemy he has killed. The enemy, however is not only a German but also that part of the English soldier who dreams of healing wounds, ending war, and shedding his uniform. The enemy maps out what he would have liked to have done had he lived:

Then, when much blood had clogged their chariot wheels,
I would go up and wash them from sweet wells,
Even with truths that lie too deep for taint.
I would have poured my spirit without stint
But not through wounds; not on the cess of war.

The gesture of washing from a well is both biblical and female as is the expending of self not as warrior but as a peacemaker.

In curious ways, Owen seems deliberately to take the stance in his poetry, too, of an observer rather than a participant. One is, then, falsely led at times to think of him as vicariously experiencing the war as an empathetic woman might, not as a commissioned officer. He writes that he returns to the Front in 1918 "to help these boys ... indirectly by *watching* their sufferings that I may speak of them as well as a pleader can." (my italics)[17] One could almost forget that Owen was a soldier himself and not a nurse. A number of poems, "Dulce," "Greater Love," "Asleep," "Futility," "A Terre," and "Mental Cases," also have the persona record events other soldiers suffer. As witness and scribe of a new text other than Abram's, he constantly identifies with the innocent victims acted upon by those far more powerful. Likewise he repeatedly turns his men into boys, into children whom he nurtures and cares for much as his influential mother nurtured him.

In subverting the father figure and his current reign, Owen will appropriate sources of female power, but he carefully excludes women from any but the most marginal existence in his re-visioned world. Like other male modernists, such as Lawrence, Eliot, and Joyce, Owen establishes a paradise populated and dominated by men. Like them, too, his passionate and most genuine bonds are with other men, but with sons, not with fathers. In critiquing the patriarch's kingdom which ostensibly he should inherit, Owen defines the king as murderous, refuses initiations into several socializing male rites, and transforms men into boys, thus recapturing their less gender-differentiated pre-pubescent state. In so doing, Owen undermines the power of Abram whom he credits with causing such carnage in the world. Although some other officer had to write "Deceased" across Owen's name on November 4, 1918, Owen's poetry, life, and letters still testify to the ways he himself sought to scrawl "Deceased" over Abram's death-laden books.

Notes

1. Wilfred Owen, *Collected Letters*, eds. Harold Owen and John Bell (London: Oxford University Press, 1967), p. 274.
2. Owen and Bell, p. 421.
3. Owen and Bell, p. 423.
4. Owen and Bell, p. 425.
5. Owen and Bell, p. 428.
6. Owen and Bell, p. 582.
7. Phillip Knightley in *The First Casualty: From the Crimea to Vietnam, The War Correspondent as Hero, Propagandist, and Myth Maker* (New York: Harcourt, Brace Jovanovich, 1975) claims of World War I, "And so began a great conspiracy. More deliberate lies were told than in any other period of history, and the whole apparatus of the state went into action to suppress the truth" (p. 80). Owen is, of course, aware of the military pressures on him to not speak the truth about the war, and as an officer one of his duties was to censor soldiers' letters home. An early letter in August, 1916, just after enlisting has a light tone as he writes home, "But, here I am beginning to 'leak information,' (when I have to read daily a solemn W.O. Letter, saying that no talk of the War is even to be indulged in, even in private letters and so on!). Owen and Bell, p. 402. In a more telling letter a month before he dies, Owen says to his mother, "If I started into detail of our engagement I should disturb the Censor and my own Rest." Owen and Bell, p. 580.
8. Wilfred Owen, *The Collected Poems of Wilfred Owen*, ed. C. Day Lewis (New York: New Directions, 1963), p. 42. All subsequent quotations from Owen's poems are taken from Lewis' edition.
9. Paul Fussell, *The Great War and Modern Memory* (London: Oxford University Press, 1975), p. 27.
10. Fussell, p. 272.
11. Fussell, p. 295.
12. That Owen had avoided heterosexual encounters before the war is implied in several letters home to his mother. In one he is talking of his sexual attraction to "good" women as well as prostitutes: "All women, without exception, *annoy* me, and the mercenaries . . . I utterly detest; more indeed than as a charitable being I ought." Owen and Bell, p. 234. Although women did not arouse Owen, he seemed to arouse them. His employer, Mme. Leger, whose daughter he tutored, apparently was interested in some sort of liaison with her young attractive

Englishman. Embarrassed and startled, Owen assures his mother of his intentions, "I am conscious that she has a considerable liking for me both in a physical and intellectual sense. She is now equally conscious that the former liking is not reciprocated — not one little bit ..." Owen and Bell, p. 279. Of his attraction for young boys, Owen was unabashed in his letters home as he describes a fifteen year old, Andre Martin, who came up to Owen and began singing: "Now his eyes, and indeed his whole countenance were the most romantically beautiful I had ever beheld." Owen and Bell, p. 288. Owen strikes up a friendship with Andre following the incident.

13. Owen and Bell, p. 449.
14. Jon Stallworthy, *Wilfred Owen: A Biography* (London: Oxford University Press, 1974), p. 28. Stallworthy is quoting from Harold Owen's *Journey From Obscurity: Wilfred Owen 1893-1918* (London: Oxford University Press, 1963), I, 103.
15. Owen and Bell, p. 581.
16. Owen's poetry contains images of divisions and fragmentation which Sandra Gilbert and Susan Gubar argue so persuasively in *The Madwoman in the Attic* (New Haven: Yale University Press, 1979) defined women's literary tradition of the nineteenth century. See also Sandra M. Gilbert's "Soldier's Heart: Literary Women, and the Great War," *Signs* 8 (Spring 1983), 422-450. Exploring the ways the Great War intensified the battle between the sexes, she argues that men, feeling themselves increasingly important, came to perceive women as menacingly powerful. It puts Owen's misogynist vein in an illuminating context.
17. Owen and Bell, p. 580.

D.H. Lawrence, World War I and the battle between the sexes: A reading of "The Blind Man" and "Tickets, Please"

JUDITH PUCHNER BREEN

San Francisco State University

"THE BLIND MAN" and "Tickets, Please," two well-known stories by D.H. Lawrence written in the fall and winter of 1918-19,[1] dramatize his ironic vision of World War I as an opportunity for the destruction of an exhausted culture and the rebirth of long-repressed erotic energies, energies embodied by the scarred and sightless Maurice Pervin in "The Blind Man," and in "Tickets, Please" by the mysterious tramway inspector John Thomas. Both Maurice and John Thomas are figures with a double identity, in some respects less characters than masks that imperfectly conceal the dark gods of pagan fertility lurking behind them. For example, when Maurice lost his eyes in Flanders, he was at once wounded by a murderously corrupt society and blessed by the recovery of the sense of touch — to Lawrence the most sacred of the senses — thereby returning to a more primitive state of psychic organization "as if he rose out of the earth."[2] In "Tickets, Please" the disruption of the home front, seen in the empowerment of the women who assume the jobs and the prerogatives of the departed soldiers, has summoned into its midst a similar god-man, the resurrected Dionysus, representative of phallic power and prophet of a revitalized culture.

The customary reading of both stories is that they dramatize

Women's Studies, 1986
Vol. 13, pp. 063-074
0049-7878/86/1302-0063 $18.50/0

conflict between this new phallic man and the surviving pre-war civilization. Thus in "The Blind Man" Maurice competes for possession of his wife, Isabel, with her dear friend and guest Bertie Reid, a successful but impotent intellectual dandy. In the end Maurice transcends this conflict in an effort to establish a bond of idealized, masculine friendship with Bertie and thus enlarge his life purpose. In "Tickets, Please" John Thomas (as type character the equivalent, in American slang, to "Peter" or "Dick") is overwhelmed by a Bacchante-like attack of enraged discarded girl friends and their leader, Annie, who seek to end his free and easy ways by forcing him to choose one sweetheart. However he snatches victory from defeat when he chooses Annie, making her sensible of the gift of rich love she has lost through her misguided possessiveness.

In this paper I am going to argue, however, that precisely the reverse takes place in each story. Beneath the manifest text lies a latent subtext, which reveals a quite different view of the battle between the sexes — a text less socially permissable, perhaps not fully acknowledged by Lawrence himself, but nevertheless expressive of his profoundest imaginings. In my reading of "The Blind Man," Isabel, the apparently sympathetic wife and friend, immersed in the last weeks of pregnancy, represents in fact the omnipotent, indifferent nature goddess to whom, in Wolfgang Lederer's words, "all man's efforts and achievements are as the games of children"[3] as she ruthlessly pursues her procreative instincts. Burdened by her husband at a time when she wishes to be able to devote herself to her infant, she sets up Maurice in a sham friendship with Bertie in order to get him off her hands. Far from being winners or losers, Bertie and Maurice are both victims of Isabel's self-interest.

If in "The Blind Man" the woman is the real winner, in "Tickets, Please" woman is forced to recognize in brutal physical terms the limits of her power. The attack of the angry women on the "cock of the walk" John Thomas has all the strange frenzy of sexual arousal; but while together they can vilify him, disrobe him, pummel him, they cannot impose the final humiliation and rape him. Only John Thomas has the power to penetrate, to choose. In the one story, then, woman at her most loving conceals her ruthless power; in the other, woman at her most aggressive conceals her fundamental impotence.

As we shall see, the single source of both these apparently irreconcilable faults is her failure to be a man.[4]

"The Blind Man" opens on a subdued but intense note of crisis. At dusk on a rainy November at the Pervin's farm, near the end of the calendar year and the year of "wonderful and unspeakable intimacy" (347) between Isabel and her husband since his blinding, Isabel listens for the sound of the trap she has sent to fetch Bertie. The impending arrival of Bertie alerts the reader to the mixed reception awaiting the other expected newcomer, the new baby. And both these anxieties provide a focus for the internal pressures that have increasingly troubled the wonderful intimacy of husband and wife during the past year. Isabel has been visited from time to time with feelings of *ennui*, of unexplained weariness, and Maurice by "devastating fits of depression" (347), which have intermittently made their life unbearable.

In the past such painful episodes have served in some ways only to underscore the profound bond between husband and wife. As Maurice works around the powerful hind-quarters of the horses in his stable, feeling the earth with his feet as he goes, he appears to Isabel "a tower of darkness" (354), some savage old earth spirit, as it were, who escaped suppression by the transcendent deities — or, as we saw earlier, the demonic Pluto who rose out of darkness to claim Persephone for his bride. However, in other ways the primitive intensity of their bond explains the depressions disturbing the married couple. The unspeakable intimacy uniting Isabel and Maurice is to be taken literally, it is an intimacy that goes beyond the genital bond of husband and wife to recover the pre-genital, language-less tie between infant and mother.[5] In this context the "unspeakable" element of the intimacy, referred to three times in the story, carries gothic hints of mother-son incest.

There is no space in the present study to discuss the many images in the story which identify Maurice as the infant-husband and focus on Isabel as the all-powerful mother whose magical maternal kisses, which once healed cuts and bruises, now heal the blind Maurice and give him his psychic and phallic strength; one example — "he did not even regret the loss of his sight in these times of dark, palpable joy. A certain exultance swelled his soul" (347) — must do. It is clear, however, that such precognitive intimacy explains Maurice's depressions, as well as his palpable joys, for the son's developing ego, childishly dependent and fearful of destruction, may be threatened as well as empowered by the mother. The mirror-image of Isabel, caught in an unguarded moment, exposes this malign as well as benign side of the wife-mother: "her grey eyes looked amused and wicked, a little sardonic, out of her transfigured Madonna face" (351).

Maurice's depression may be caused as well by the constraining domesticity of his wife, by, as Mark Spilka has suggested in a well-known study,[6] her wish to tie him to the "sphere of connubial felicity," letting "everything else fade into insignificance" (349). However both these fears of engulfment and constraint are adumbrated in the overwhelming anxiety which dominates Maurice in the story, the fear of abandonment. It is as if through Isabel's pregnancy the blind man were wounded once more, damaged more profoundly by the war between the sexes than the war between the nations. For Lawrence presents Isabel in her maternity as sinking back into the deep sleep from which Maurice had awakened her: on the one hand she is a hostile Beauty who wishes to get rid of her Prince Charming and go back to bed ("Maurice was like an ominous thundercloud. She had to keep waking up to remember him") (350); on the other hand she is a fleeing Persephone who wishes to be "snatched away off the earth" (348) that has enfolded her, to flee the dark cavern and return to the world of time and change, to the surface of life, in her role of mother, as it is conventionally lived. To formulate this dilemma in a slightly different way which underscores Lawrence's remarkable hostility to pregnancy in the story: Isabel has been defeated by Maurice's resistance to her desire to "possess her husband utterly" (348); now she longs to replace him with the infant she can completely possess. Bertie in the story functions in part as a surrogate for this other, more threatening visitor, who creates not an inclination but a compulsion within Isabel to reject the glory of what Lawrence calls "blood-consciousness" and fade into the light of common day.

This family romance is carefully delineated through the architectural details of the Pervin's house, particularly the twisting corridors, suggestive of the umbilical cord, which connect the front rooms, Isabel's domain, to the back rooms housing the resident farmer's family, and then to the narrow causeway leading to Maurice's territory, the dark, vibrant stable.[7] Symbolic interchanges between stable and domestic quarters, as if the farmstead in between were a changing room, mark crucial stages in the story. Maurice travels twice from the barn to the front rooms, where the pungency of the living horses is replaced by the fragrance of *potpourri*, traditional talisman against the odors of the flesh. On the first visit Maurice sits like a sculptured monument during the uncomfortable dinner with Isabel and Bertie. In a gesture recalling the cowardly fop in Shakespeare's *1 Henry IV* who enraged Hotspur by raising a pouncet box between his nose and the stench of battle, Bertie, "without knowing what he did" (368), raised a bowl of violets to his nose to deflect the terrible force of Maurice's wounds. On this occasion Maurice is soon defeated by Bertie's evasions and returns to the barn. However on his second trip to the house, as we shall see, Maurice feels that his influence triumphs.

Maurice's movements are bracketed by two corresponding visits from house to barn. The first is by Isabel, who anxiously goes to check on her husband in preparation for Bertie's arrival. Before crossing the cold causeway, half-relishing, half-fearing the stormy blasts to be met there, she dons a figure-masking shawl and a man's felt hat. With this gesture she manages the transition from the world of book reviews to the "strange swirl of violent life" (353) she finds in the darkness, the almost mesmerizing power of the god she both creates and serves. But at the end of the story Isabel forgoes a second visit. Because she "did not want to make the physical effort" (362), she sends Bertie to meet Maurice in her place.

What is the reader to make of this psychological traffic pattern? Unlike his Victorian predecessors, who divided women into angels or demons, Lawrence divides them into angels and demons, dubbing the frightening half of their sexuality "female," and the nurturing side which magnifies the male, "masculine." From this point of view Isabel's function in the story, when she wears the man's hat, is to mask Maurice's longing for a more perfect union — a union with a man. This explains Maurice's conduct when Isabel sends Bertie on the second trip to the barn. Now that Isabel's pregnancy has stilled her masculine passions, Maurice seizes the opportunity to replace her.

From Maurice's point of view, the attempt to substitute Isabel's friend for Isabel has clear advantages. His fingers rove sensitively over the face of Bertie just as they did in an earlier scene over the face of Isabel, performing a ritual reenactment of infant-mother bonding that allows him to maintain his heroic stature; at the end of the story he swells to a "colossus" (365). When Maurice compels Bertie to explore his face in turn, he is living out a fantasy of male union in which he entirely circumvents the need for women so that he can become self-created, the author of his own powers.

But what of Bertie's enforced role in this fantasy? Ironically, Bertie has been sent to do a man's job when he is more deficient in this regard than Isabel; whereas she merely showed ambivalence in crossing the yard to the barn, Bertie "shrank from the wet and roaring night" (362). Though he starts out to meet Maurice with his man's hat on, it is soon knocked off when the groping Maurice significantly misjudges his height. This weakness causes the ceremony of mutual bonding to short-circuit, and all unknowingly Maurice is left with a second sham marriage. Nevertheless Maurice's effort does look forward to a time when male brotherhood will pre-empt heterosexual marriage. If the damaged warrior does not arrive there, at least one barrier, Bertie's false intellect, has been crushed like the shell of a mollusk.

And what of Isabel? At the end of the story she knows Maurice can believe in his friendship with Bertie only because he is blind, and she knows Bertie suffers agonies from his encounter with Maurice. But she purrs contentedly to her husband, "You'll be happier now, dear" (365), meaning instead that she'll be happier now Maurice is off her hands. In this final picture of Isabel, then, her false mask and the true image reflected in the mirror coalesce. Apparently all sympathy and kindness, she views with complacent indifference the consequences of the trap she set for Bertie, gladly sacrificing both husband and friend to the new life within her womb.

"Tickets, Please" shares with "The Blind Man" the same Lawrentian antinomies of the dark god and a sterile culture. But in this story, as if to emphasize his rejection of conventional love plots, Lawrence parodies the conventions of romantic love comedy, in which lovers typically meet in the world of an oppressive everyday; escape to a world of holiday where nature reigns, law relaxes, and the barriers to happiness are overcome; and return transformed to a purged and elevated everyday world.[8] In "Tickets, Please," though, there is no everyday, only a homefront disrupted by the departure for the trenches of all able-bodied men and the substitution of women, along with "cripples and hunchbacks" (334), in their jobs as conductors on a tram line connecting villages and coal mines in the industrial country-side of central England. Moreover, as no everyday world remains, no clearly-contrasting holiday world exists either. When the action of the story shifts from the tram line to the Statutes Fair at nearby Bestwood, Annie finds her ride on the Dragons cozy, because of John Thomas's encircling arm, but less exciting than the plunging, tilting tram car. The circular rides the pair enjoy on the roundabout alert the reader to the equally futile motions of the trams shuttling back and forth to Terminus, past the industrial town which provides for the life-weary miners the meaningless stimulation of "a change of cinema, of girls, of pub" (335).

There is finally no movement from everyday to holiday in Lawrence's story because there is no sense of place in it at all, as Jane Austen or George Eliot meant it, not even the stable stable which fosters Maurice's rooted strength; the only roots Annie is to know is her "rich, warm" (339) place in John Thomas's arms. But if holiday is just a continuation of everyday, then of course nothing can be learned, and the palpable joy John Thomas offers loses its transforming power. The "intelligent interest" (339) Annie begins to take in him, despite her full return of his passion, represents her inability to relinquish the possessive ways her culture has instilled. As the concluding battle between the sexes shows, for Lawrence the defeat of such an offspring of Rosamond Vincy is the only possible happy ending to love plots in the industrial age.

At the beginning of "Tickets, Please," however, the dynamics of this mock love story are not absolutely fixed. When in the opening pages Lawrence describes his conductresses in their short-skirted uniforms and peaked caps as "fearless young hussies" (335) who pounce on sneaky youths and tread on the toes of howling colliers, he seems to admire the new bread of masculinized women the way he admired the masculine energies of Isabel. If these new women remain linked to ominous hints of petticoat government, the reckless swoops of their trams are linked as well to infernal energies, their trail of sparks to the fire and brimstone in which Shaw as well as Lawrence saw the

salvation of the modern world. But these new women lack fit suitors —
the colliers on their run are indoor types who, like Bertie, shrink from
the howlingly cold nights — until their very need seems magically to
summon forth John Thomas, representing the rare presence of
sensual power in modern culture.[9]

As inspector of trams, this mythological John Thomas comes and
goes by profession; as a type of fertility god he does so by inclination,
and has his way with many of the working girls. His clothing — black
overcoat buttoned up to the chin, tweed cap pulled down over the eyes
— functions as a traditional stage disguise, wittily recalling the
disguised royalty of Shakespeare's wartime king, Henry V, who also
passed unrecognized as he revitalized his weary flock. The self-
possessed Annie Stone, tired of the boy she has on the string, responds
to the persuasive ways of this skillful lover, and John Thomas rightly
prefers her above all others for "the soft, melting way in which she
could flow into a fellow" (339). The tactile images of interpenetration
and suffusion in their love scenes recall the unspeakable intimacy of
Maurice and Isabel.

However, Annie's kinship to Isabel suggests that her true mate
really is her discarded boy-friend, as does the comedy of her rational-
izations for yielding to John Thomas. For example, he is "discreet,"
and like a current fashion comes in the "right style" (337); "he paid
each time so she could be but complaisant" (338); and on her ride on
the merry-go-round with a "perfectly happy" (338) John Thomas, she
divides her attention between her lover and her crooked hat. This
conflict between love and vanity in Annie, and the materialistic
overtones of her language, explain her possessiveness and, in the end,
her passion for revenge. When John Thomas falls short on what she
considers their bargain, she makes her choice, and in an act of self-
reification she "determine[s] to have her own back" (339).

The trap Annie sets for John Thomas in the ladies waiting room at
Terminus is the same trap Isabel set for her prey in the Grange; both
use food, warmth and the charm of feminine culture to disguise their
monstrous cunning. However John Thomas participates more in his
own undoing than Maurice, who has been blinded by a corrupt war
and a pregnant wife. John Thomas is self-blinding, and betrays his
realm, the world of dark and lawless nature, for the flattering company

of female admirers. But in Lawrence's comparison of John Thomas to some sort of swamp beast crawling out of the damp to sun himself, he shows that John Thomas's self-destructive urge to ravin down his bane is irresistable. Man is an amphibian in Lawrence's story, native to worlds of light and darkness. It is as natural to John Thomas to seek warmth — though a king, he suffers want like other men — as it is for the swamp beast, even though, with cloak doffed and hat recklessly pushed back in the warm waiting room, like the beast he exposes himself to peril.

The girls' revenge begins playfully but not randomly; after turning John Thomas's face to the wall, one after the other taps him on the back to see if he can tell one girl from another in the dark. But when Annie steps forward, taps turn to blows; she gives a smart box to John Thomas's head that sends his hat flying and stirs up the buried aggression of her followers, who are transformed into strange wild creatures hunting down a terrified animal. For the hatless man in this story is not, like Bertie, a sexless creature; the stripping away of his clothes (the "sight of his white, bare arm maddened the girls" [344]) stirs his attackers into a sexual frenzy. Like the Bacchantes, in their possession of the god they are "filled with supernatural strength" (344).

This possession of the body of John Thomas has other implications as well, and Annie, as she kneels on his back in a reversal of the traditional missionary position, asserts the ascendency of her sex and assumes for herself the patriarchal right to force the seducer to marry: "'You've got to choose,' she cried" (344). In this assumption of male sexual perogatives, despite a secret misgiving because "she could not exact more" (344), she appears to win the battle of the sexes.

Yet John Thomas "did not give in to them really — no, not if they tore him to bits" (344); he jerks his face loose from Annie's grasp and, in a voice "strange and full of malice," utters the words "I choose Annie" (344). Instantly Annie collapses in "bitter hopelessness" (345) and commands the girls to end their taunts. John Thomas's victory rests on her realization that while she can force him to the ground, only he can "exact more," and his choice of Annie vindictively reminds her of the realities of sexual politics. At the end of the story, then, Annie is not horrified because (as sentimental readers might feel) she has lost invaluable love through her possessive ways; rather "something" (her assumed masculine power, we can guess) "is broken in her" (345), and she is tormented by her realization that she is too weak to wreak vengeance on her enemy. Male genital power, says Lawrence, is the final power.

If the title "Tickets, Please" suggests to many readers Lawrence's habitual misogyny — man pays a price to get in the gate — it also suggests a more fundamental, more disturbing point: no matter how strengthened by the freedoms brought by World War I, women can never be the equals of men. The source of their power remains in the underlining of the word *please*. Annie's essential failure in her own eyes — the most cruel element in her humiliation — as well as in those of John Thomas, is her failure to be a man. Beaten but undefeated, John Thomas reassembles the cloak and cap of his stage disguise. Annie herself produces the key to unlock the door of the escape, and he returns alone to his mist-filled darkness to await a better day.

What conclusions may be drawn from reading "The Blind Man" and "Tickets, Please" in conjunction? First of all, the brutal humiliation of Annie Stone, which is pushed beyond anything that buoyant heroine actually merits in the story (and helps earn for Lawrence his reputation with some readers as misogynist) can best be understood as a response to the remarkable inflation of Isabel's powers. Lawrence focuses so intently in his fiction on the shortcomings of women because underneath that fantasy lies a far more terrifying fantasy, especially intolerable to the male artist, a fantasy which magnifies women's creative and life-giving strengths. One of Lawrence's primary gifts as a writer is his ability to discover and dramatize such hidden plots, which are in fiction so compelling, and in real life so destructive to women.

Second, Lawrence's glance back to Shakespeare's Henriad in "The Blind Man" and "Tickets, Please" reveals a nostalgia for the heroic possibilities of war, possibilities including Hotspur's celebration of his smarting wounds as the badge of manliness, and the sign of the willingness to take on directly the best and worst life has to offer. "The patriarchal world of Shakespeare's history plays is emphatically masculine," Coppélia Kahn has written. John Thomas, like Lawrence himself, expends his creative forces on the home front. But the proper setting for the majestic presence he conceals behind hat and overcoat was originally the military world of "simple, idealized male comradships" characteristic of *King Henry V*, and free of feminine influence.[10]

Finally, this reading of "A Blind Man" and "Tickets, Please" suggests an important area of investigation for feminist critics. As Sandra M. Gilbert and Susan Gubar have argued in *The Madwoman in the Attic*,[11] consciously or unconsciously women novelists frequently express unacceptable feelings such as anger or passion through the use of doubles and other encoding devices. So too in these stories Lawrence has encoded his secret plot of homosexual love within the parameters of more permissible plots. Whether or not his strategy can be generalized to the works of other male writers is beyond the scope of this study. E.M. Forster, for example, chose to suppress *Maurice* entirely. But "The Blind Man" and "Tickets, Please" do suggest the value of a comparative analysis of the techniques used by male and female writers for expressing subversive themes in literature.

Notes

1. I have followed the dating of Keith Sagar, *The Art of D. H. Lawrence* (Cambridge, England: Cambridge University Press, 1966), p. 99, who assigns "The Blind Man" to November 1918, somewhat before "Tickets, Please" (fall and winter of 1918-19) — though "Tickets, Please" was published more than a year earlier.
2. Lawrence, P. 354. Page references (hereafter cited in the text) are to D.H. Lawrence, *The Complete Short Stories*, vol. II (Harmondsworth, Middlesex, England: Penguin Books Ltd, 1976) as the most widely available edition.
3. *The Fear of Women* (New York: Harcourt Brace Jovanovich, 1968), p. 142.
4. For my approach to "The Blind Man" and "Tickets, Please" I am indebted to participants in the NEH Summer Seminar "Feminism, Modernism, and Feminist Criticism" at the University of California, Davis in 1981 — and most especially to its co-directors, Sandra M. Gilbert and Susan Gubar, whose invaluable suggestions and encouragement I gratefully acknowledge.
5. See the connection between the unspeakably direct love of infant and blind man made by Lawrence himself in *Psychoanalysis of the Unconscious*, written Dec-Jan 1919-20, about a year after "The Blind Man:"

    And from the cardiac plexus goes forth that strange effluence of the self which seeks and dwells upon the beloved, lovingly roving like the fingers of an infant or a blind man over the face of the treasured object, gathering her mold forever into its own deep unconscious psyche. This is the first acquiring of objective knowledge, sightless, unspeakably direct. It is a dwelling of the child's unconscious within the form of the mother, the gathering of a pure, eternal impression.

6. *The Love Ethic of D.H. Lawrence* (Bloomington: Indiana University Press, 1955), p. 299.
7. The ironic equivalent of the umbilical cord for the intellect is the mail route out the front door and down the straight and narrow avenue to the road along which Isabel sends her book reviews to the Edinburgh newspapers.
8. See the well-known discussions by Northrop Frye in *Anatomy of Criticism: Four Essays* (Princeton, New Jersey: Princeton University Press, 1957), pp. 163-86 and C.L. Barber in *Shakespeare's Festive Comedy* (Princeton, New Jersey: Princeton University Press, 1959), chapter 1.
9. Note however that not all the girls fare equally. Cissy Meakin, whose name declares her a meek and weak sissy under the thumb of her mother, is forced to quit her job. The turnover rate among the conductresses does seem rather high. Some succumb to their alert mothers, apparently, some to pregnancy.
10. Coppélia Kahn, *Man's Estate* (Berkeley: University of California Press, 1981), p. 81.
11. New Haven, Connecticut: Yale University Press, 1979.

On the battlefield: Vera Brittain's *Testament of Youth*

JEAN PICKERING

Department of English, CSU-Fresno

With scientific precision, I studied the memoirs of Blunden, Sassoon, and Graves. Surely, I thought, my story is as interesting as theirs? Besides, I see things other than they have seen, and some of the things they perceive I see differently.[1]

THUS IN 1929 Vera Brittain prepared to write her autobiography of the war years, *Testament of Youth.* "Why," she asked, "should these young men have the war all to themselves?" (TE, 77). The picture of women they presented as only "suffering wives and mothers, or callous parasites, or mercenary prostitutes" by no means told the whole story. She therefore intended to write for the whole generation of idealistic young women who had, she felt, sacrificed as much as the men with far less recognition. Her explicit aim was, in Gilbert's and Gubar's words, to "valorize female nature and culture."[2]

Brittain's autobiography was to some extent a response to the already published memoirs of Blunden, Sassoon, and Graves. All four of these books were written so long after the war that the authors had had time to assimilate their experience to traditional literary patterns. At the moment of occurrence, the traumatic incidents must have been chaotic for eyewitnesses, who needed to exert the pressure of the mind and of the years in order to reduce them to some kind of meaning. Paul Fussell has pointed out that Blunden's *Undertones of War* is patterned on the pastoral elegy,[3] Sassoon's *Memoirs of a Fox-Hunting Man* on the

Women's Studies, 1986
Vol. 13, pp. 075-085
0049-7878/86/1302-0075 $18.50/0

pastoral romance (F, 94), both relying on the juxtaposition of literary form and war experience to make an ironic contrast. In Graves's *Goodbye to All That* the ironic function is explicit, for the memoir takes the form of a farce (F, 203), a Comedy of Humors as in Ben Jonson (F, 204). Graves himself was highly aware of this function: his memories, he said, presented themselves as caricature scenes. Brittain's *Testament of Youth* is built on the structure of romantic comedy, ending, after the years of grief and isolation, in the traditional comic conclusion of marriage.

Each of these texts has a distinctive surface metaphor for society: Blunden, the shepherd's solitary watch; Sassoon, the fox hunt; Graves, the public school; Brittain, the dinner or tea party. All of them, however, are informed by what Fussell calls "binary vision" (p. 82). The habit of dividing the world into "us" and "them" carried over from the trenches so that "they" were others besides the Germans. "They" might be at the base instead of up the line; indeed, "they" might well be the entire civilian population. In short, the image of the battlefield underlies all four memoirs and provides a common metaphor.

How much, then, did this binary vision affect the world view of Vera Brittain, who came to adulthood just as the war began? I suspect that it affected her view not only of the war and of subsequent years, but also her memories of the years leading up to them. The very first sentence of *Testament of Youth* mentions the effect that the war had on her. All the childhood incidents she recalls point forward to those events, particularly the death of Roland, that determined the course of her life. Thus the image of the battlefield shadows her entire autobiography. This binary vision structured not only the way she perceived herself in opposition to her father, to the administrations of Oxford University and of the VAD, but also her understanding of the contrast between her youthful outlook at the time when the events took place and her mature outlook at the time of writing.

With her dichotomizing vision strengthened, if not actually caused, by the war, Brittain felt a strong competitive urge when she came to write her autobiography. The male memoirists were already in print before she visualized her plan, so her work clearly stands in a dialectical relationship to theirs. Unlike the men, who said very little about the opposite sex, she took pains to detail her relationships with a number of male figures, thus establishing a dialectic within the book as well as between it and the memoirs already published. Her disagreements with her father and with Roland were pronounced, but because her overriding feelings for these figures were affectionate, as they unambiguously were for Edward, her real battle was against the tradition of authority, and this she waged regardless of whether the seat of power was occupied by man or woman.

Although she tried to indicate her youthful outlook by including letters, diary entries, and poems, her outlook at the time of writing predominates. The battlefield had become, as for her contemporaries, an image which structured the way she looked at the world. The battle she perceived between the claims of the private life and the public life, which I take to be the overall concern of *Testament of Youth*, was powered by the psychological mind set imprinted on her entire generation. The polarity between the two spheres was, I think, much more apparent to the woman of 1929 than it had been to the girl of 1914.

The separation of the public from the private life was, if not caused, at least exacerbated by the Industrial Revolution, with its removal of work from the home and by the nineteenth century flight to suburbia, with the ensuing need to disguise both through propaganda and through conspicuous consumption the fact that women's sphere of activity had, by the end of the Victorian period, been severely curtailed. Brittain's autobiography shows a reversal of this trend: raised to be a lady, she nonetheless fought her way into Oxford, worked for four years as a military nurse, and carved out a career as a writer and lecturer on feminist, pacifist, and socialist issues. In addition, she maintained a transatlantic commuter marriage: her husband, George Catlin, for many years taught every other semester at Cornell. Thus she managed to integrate the public and the private into the fabric of a satisfying life.

The private life treasured by the Victorians had, however, little to do with personal privacy, and though Victorian values generally declined during the Edwardian age, Brittain's provincial upbringing continued to emphasize the role of woman as the guardian of domestic emotions. Daughters in particular had no privacy away from the family; during Roland's courtship, Brittain felt the weight, not of parental disapproval, but of parental interest because parents "regarded it as a bounden duty to speak their minds at every tentative stage of a developing love affair".[4] Furthermore, the activities and emotions of daughters were thoroughly supervised and "openly discussed in the family circle: their correspondence was monitored and commented on" (TY, 120).

The private life of women complementing the public life of men was thus not a personal life but a domestic life. And it was for this kind of existence that Brittain was trained, though hardly in a special way. She grew up knowing nothing of household management, for her father was determined that she "should be turned into an entirely ornamental young lady" (TY, 32). Her upbringing as a sensitive plant, however, had no more profound effect on her than dismay at the level of comfort at Oxford, for which, Woolf not having yet publicized the poverty of the women's colleges, she was unprepared. And yet her father, who was the prime force behind this unsuitable training, was her childhood champion for reasons which the reader is quick enough to see: temperamentally she was much like him, more so than Edward, her brother, who took after his mother's family. Brittain pointed out that her father was determined to have Edward succeed him in the family business though she was herself much more suited to this kind of managerial position. Her father's early support may have made her all the more bitter when she realized her second class status. Certainly her resentment was life-long: "probably no ambitious girl who has lived in a family which regards the subservience of women as part of the natural order of creation ever recovers from the bitterness of her early emotions" (TY, 59). She grew up in a culture which regarded "young women as perpetually at the disposal of husbands or fathers" (TY, 261). Even when she was serving as a nurse in a front line hospital her father wrote to her that "as your mother and I can no longer manage without you, it is your duty to leave France immediately and return to Kensington" (TY, 241). Though Brittain resented this directive, she had problems of conscience when she struggled against the precepts she had unwillingly assimilated. The language of her analysis indicates that she saw the issue as a feminist one: men do not generally find themselves with family, duty, and conscience ranged against profession, ambition, and achievement. This alignment, of course, follows the private — public axis with the preferred values for women falling on the side of private life.

Brittain's first attempt to escape the domestic restrictions of Buxton took the form of trying to establish a larger life for herself. At this stage, she still saw her difficulty as that of an isolated individual, and regarded, as so many young women did and do, a higher education as the way out of her provincial young ladyhood. She managed at length to persuade her father to let her go to Oxford, "the sound cash value" (TY, 76) of the exhibition she won having convinced him. At the last minute he reneged in a fury at the outbreak of World War I, which, he maintained, would send them all to the workhouse. Thus Brittain's first reaction was that the war was "an interruption of the most exasperating kind to [her] personal plans" (TY, 17). Her own battles to establish a personal as opposed to a domestic life were of more immediate importance to her: having fought her father so long for the privilege of going to college only to have it threatened by forces far away from her daily life impressed on her a lesson she never forgot: "no life is really private."

The very typicality of her life prompted her to write the autobiography she intended "to speak ... for my generation of obscure young women" (TE, 77). The moral imagination that allowed her to see her own experience as a paradigm for that of a whole generation was not easily acquired, but learned from hard lessons. Though she noticed in her early years that girls' lives were much more restricted than boys', her affection for her brother and his complementary support prevented her from experiencing personal jealousy. Her feelings of distress therefore assumed a general anger against the lot of women, even though few of her mother's generation seemed to object to their lot. This generalizing tendency, probably because of the binary vision she developed in response to the war, became an established pattern: her reactions to her circumstances never remained purely personal but created the basis for her larger concerns. Because her beliefs were grounded in her own experience, her personal and her public attitudes were all of a piece, which resulted in an extraordinary integrity.

The feminism which, aroused by her family circumstances, prompted Brittain to work for a place at Oxford also sent her into nursing with the VAD. This activity had a personal basis: during "three radiant days of July 1914" (TY,87) — "the one perfect summer idyll [she] ever experienced" (TY, 91) — she fell "more deeply and ardently in love than [she] had ever been or [was] ever likely to be" (TY, 121) with Roland Leighton, her brother's friend, a "brilliant, reserved, extravagant personality" (p. 114). Like most of his class and generation, he volunteered early in the war, persistently applying for a commission until he at last managed to get one with the Norfolk Territorials in October of 1914. His frame of mind, so typical of the public school boy at the beginning of the war, is clearly indicated in a letter he wrote to Vera:

I feel that I am meant to take an active part in this War. It is to me a very fascinating thing — something, if often horrible, yet very ennobling and very beautiful, something whose elemental reality raises it above the reach of all cold theorising. You will call me a militarist. You may be right (TY, 104).

From the very first, Vera's love for Roland was colored by the fear of losing him. Before he went to France, he promised her that, if he died there, "he would try to come back and tell [her] that the grave was not the end of [their] love" (TY, 130). Her anxiety for his life was further compounded by "a new fear that the War would come between [them] — as indeed, with time, the War always did, putting a barrier of indescribable experience between men and the women whom they loved, thrusting horror deeper and deeper inward, linking the dread of spiritual death to the apprehension of physical disaster" (TY, 143).

Hard as she had worked for a place at Oxford, she now determined to ask for a leave of absence to become a nurse — the nearest female equivalent of Roland's military service. Yet she had little of the patriotic fervor animating the first male volunteers, the most famous spokesman for which was Rupert Brooke, already dead in the Aegean, whose outlook contrasted wildly with the poets at the end of the war when the writers in the trenches had begun to understand the scale of the casualties and the folly of the generals sending them to France to die in the mud. Unlike Roland, Vera was not motivated by abstract notions of glory. In her diary she recorded her real reason for volunteering for Red Cross Service: "He has to face far worse things than any sight or act I could come across; he can bear it — and so can I" (TY, 154). Her feminism implied a total egalitarianism; from the first she accepted the drawbacks as well as the advantages her philosophical position entailed. She risked her comfort, even her life, in support of a principle drawn ultimately from her own experience.

She realized that "public events and private lives had become inseparable" (TY, 98); she never forgot it. Her commitment, first to pacifism, then to socialism, came about because of her personal involvement in the war, both her vicarious experience of life in the trenches through Roland, and her own direct participation when she nursed Tommies and Huns with the most appalling injuries. The sheer physical waste of war was more apparent to her than to the policy makers who, at some remove from the actual, dealt in national honor. They, of course, were shielded from the knowledge of conditions in the trenches, as was the general public, from whom the news was deliberately kept, much to the ironic amusement of the men in France, who received the daily papers from England but whose letters home were strictly censored.

The number of maimed and dying who passed through Brittain's hands impressed upon her what it took civilians years to grasp: that her own losses were representative of those suffered by her entire generation. She lost everyone of her own generation dear to her — Roland, Geoffrey, Victor, and, in the last months of the war, her brother Edward, the loss of whom "made life itself seem unreal" (TY,444). Cut off from her contemporaries she felt entirely alone, as though their deaths had invalidated her past. At this point her sense of the personal merged into the life of the nation and of the world and never again separated from them.

A recent review of her war diary maintained that Brittain needed to believe that Roland, who provided a focus for her scattered ambitions, was perfect.[5] Her natural tendency to overlook faults in the beloved was reinforced by the emotional climate of war, one of the main casualties of which is ambiguity (F, 105). She desperately needed something to believe in, and she had faith in his heroism, which, because of the contrast with her own terrible eyewitness accounts — the deaths, the mutilations, the descents into madness and despair — has not worn well. Characters like Roland now appear only in historical novels or science fiction; the ironic bias of contemporary thought persisting from the experiences of the First World War (F, 105) makes it impossible to use them in serious fiction or to see them in life.

Her socialism, like her feminism and her pacifism, grew out of direct experience. When she returned to Oxford in 1919, she read history instead of English, thinking it more important to know the reasons leading to the outbreak of war than to study literary master-pieces. When she went down, she planned a life of part time lecturing in order to practice the writing she had always considered her vocation. She became a regular lecturer for the League of Nations, which gave her "acquaintances belonging to every social class from earls to dustmen" (TY, 568). Through this work she was drawn into national politics, though her interest was primarily international, and so became a Liberal, working for a candidate for Bethnal Green in the 1923 election. For the first time she came into "intimate contact with the homes of the poor" (TY, 575) and understood in a moment of poignant revelation the kinship between them and the Tommies she had nursed during the war. The experience made her politically minded once and for all; for the rest of her life she was committed to changing the system responsible for the misery of the poor. Eventually she joined the Labour Party and committed her energies to socialism, a political view passed on to her daughter Shirley Williams, a Laborite from adolescence until 1981 when she helped found the breakaway Social Democratic Party, of which she became the first member elected to Parliament in November of that year.

As Brittain's private concerns expressed themselves in her public life, so her public interests affected the course of her personal life. After Roland's death, she had intended sacrificially to marry Victor, blinded at Arras, but when he died of the wound that cost him his eyes, she invested all her remaining vitality in the demands of a public life. Then George Catlin, whom she did not remember meeting while they were both at Oxford after the war, began to write to her, increasing his attempts to make her acquaintance after she had published her first novel, *The Dark Tide*. Their correspondence revealed that they had political ideals in common, but because he had taken a post at

Cornell, they did not meet for almost a year. Just before he was to return to England, she began to feel that she did not want to meet him, "for a new, unwanted agitation had crept into life" (TY, 613). Her good friend, Winifred Holtby, remarked that one must choose between stagnation and agitation in this world. Had her suitor been less persistent, Vera might have chosen stagnation. Still attached to her past, she wrote, "I felt reluctant and afraid; I did not wish to live, emotionally, any more, for I was still too tired; I wanted only to stand aside from life and write" (TY, 615). This new relationship seemed a betrayal not only of Roland but of all the companions she had lost. This is the sense that afflicts survivors, making it difficult to rebuild a life: remembrance confers a kind of immortality on the dead, and to forget them denies that they ever lived. Yet she understood that to commit oneself to the living always entails breaking faith with the dead. This she knew she had to do if she was to succeed in the causes she had taken on as her life's work.

Testament of Youth ends at "a new beginning." Established as a feminist, a socialist, and a writer, Brittain is about to marry George Catlin — a feminist, a pacifist, a socialist, and a professor. This marriage reconciled not only the claims of the public and the private life but also, in some murky psychological fashion, jumped the gap between past and future by fulfilling the prophecy of the last poem Roland wrote, "Another Stranger." Resembling the "lovely companionship" Vera had enjoyed with Edward as closely as the fervor of the few ardent hours she had managed to spend with Roland, it merged her two most important lost relationships; though the remaining void was life-long, marriage to George meant immersing herself in the stream of time instead of remaining marooned in the past. Thus Brittain entered history. Writing *Testament of Youth* was a therapeutic act, allowing her to put the past behind her and devote her life to the interests of survivors and future generations.

The three other memoirists, however, were never able to reconcile their past and the present, their public and their private lives. Just before his death, Blunden wrote, "My experiences in the First World War have haunted me all my life and for many days I have, it seemed, lived in that world rather than this" (F, 256). As Fussell demonstrates, his poetry provides obvious evidence of the truth of this estimate (F, 256). The persona presented in *Undertones of War*, which focuses on the experiences of Blunden's battalion rather than on his own, does not accomodate the personal. In the "Preliminary" he specifies that the voice within him is "perhaps not his own." Sassoon was also trapped in the past: by 1945 he had spent two decades writing his memoirs of the years to 1920 (F, 92). He himself commented on his "queer craving to revisit the past and give the modern world the slip" (F. 92). In *Memoirs of a Fox-Hunting Man*, the only volume published before Brittain began *Testament of Youth*, he fictionalizes his memories by falsifying a character for himself, thus dealing with his private life by ignoring it. Graves likewise, though not so obviously fixed in the past as Blunden and Sassoon — indeed, the very title of *Good-bye to All That* implies a therapeutic farewell — has never established a footing in history. His work on the White Goddess is a caricature of mythological research in precisely the same way that his autobiography is a carica-ture of a war memoir, while his historical novels and his poetry are set in a gone world. As for his private life, he simply ignored the problem of reconciling it with his public life. At the age of four he had become aware of the distinctions in rank which would determine the course of his life; later he learned to "masquerade as a gentleman."[6] The struc-tures of the public school, echoed in the organization of the army, influenced his character in such a profound way that he seems to have altogether lost a sense of the private self.

Unlike Brittain, these three male memoirists seem to have had trouble reconciling the past with the present, and the private with the public life. Her integration of the private and the public ultimately appears to depend on her sense of self in history. The men took it for granted that they were isolated but valuable individuals; Brittain, whose plan to write "a kind of autobiography" was greeted by the exclamation that 'I shouldn't have thought anything in your life was worth recording!" (TE, 79), counted on the typicality of her experience to make it important. Seeing herself as a representative of her generation of young women did not, however, diminish her sense of individual worth; rather, it prompted an integration of the private with the public so complete that in her case the conventional division seems arbitrary.

Notes

1. Vera Brittain, *Testament of Experience* (1957; rpr., London: Fontana, 1980), p. 77. all subsequent references are to this edition.
2. Sandra Gilbert and Susan Gubar, *The Madwoman in the Attic* (New Haven: Yale University Press, 1979), p. 33.
3. *The Great War and Modern Memory* (1975; rpr., New York: Oxford University Press, 1981), p. 254. All subsequent references are to this edition.
4. Vera Brittain, *Testament of Youth* (1933; rpr., New York: Wideview, 1980), p. 180. All subsequent references are to this edition.
5. Paul Delany, "Playing Fields, Flanders Fields" *London Review of Books*, IV, 1 (21 January to 3 February, 1982), p. 22.
6. Robert Graves, *Good-bye to All That* (1929; rpt., New York: Doubleday, 1957), p. 11.

Legends of Lil: The repressed thematic center of *The Waste Land*[1]

EILEEN WIZNITZER

Department of English, University of Massachusetts

LIL OF T.S. Eliot's "A Game of Chess," the woman whose image is juxtaposed with that of the sexually alluring but abstaining "lady of situations," is something of an anomaly in *The Waste Land*. Unlike the other women directly referred to in Eliot's long poem, Lil is the only female wedded to a man and, most importantly, she is the only biologically fertile woman in an otherwise sterile land. Lil "has had five already and nearly died of young George." With this feature in mind, I will argue that Lil takes on unique significance in *The Waste Land*, a significance that has thus far either been ignored or represssed by Eliot's critics.

The very act of reimagining Lil and, by extension, the other women who appear in Eliot's nightmarish poem requires us to first remember that simply, but not only, *The Waste Land* is about the sterility of both a land and its people.[2] As we journey through the poem we find that it does not merely concede or ask its readers to concede to this sterility, a sterility that seems to be leading to a decline and disintegration of hegemonic culture.[3] Rather, the text encourages readers to explore various conventional means of regeneration: an atavistic looking to the past, mystical systems of meaning-making, heterosexual love, heterosexual and homosexual sex, religious schemas, and even the idea of the journey itself. In the end, however, the process of *The Waste Land* is a process whereby the text urges readers to deconstruct each of the conventional meaning-making structures noted above.[4] Finally,

Women's Studies, 1986
Vol. 13, pp. 087-102
0049-7878/86/1302-0087 $18.50/0

the meaning of *The Waste Land* cannot be generated through these conventional structures. *The Waste Land* remains waste; "fragments" are "shored against" an unnamed speaker's "ruins."

However, at the same time that *The Waste Land* encourages us to deconstruct traditional meaning-making structures, it urges us to recognize its innumerable gaps. The poem's broken narrative structure, its incessant use of allusion, and its over-determined diction continuously suggest empty poetic spaces. Among other things, these gaps symbolize the refusal of *The Waste Land*, as text, to create meaning and thus they mark the text's transference of the power of naming to its readers. As we read the text and respond to its structure and diction, a structure and diction that celebrate absence, we are free either to remain silent or, instead, to create meanings and to project those meanings into the text's porous framework. By choosing the former, readers reenact the high modernist "nothing" that is named by Eliot's "lady of situations" and one of his three Thames Maidens, that is pronounced by Shakespeare's Cordelia even before them, and that is suggested by the porous structure of *The Waste Land*.

'What is that noise?'
          The wind under the door.
'What is that noise now? What is the wind doing?'
          Nothing again nothing.
'You know nothing? Do you see nothing? Do you remember
    'Nothing?'

                                                        ("A Game of Chess")

'On Margate Sands.
I can connect
Nothing with nothing.
The broken fingernails of dirty hands.
My people humble people who expect
Nothing.'

                                                        ("The First Sermon")

However, by choosing to reimagine and recreate meaning and to project those meanings into the framework of *The Waste Land*, readers regenerate language and the text and thus, according to Eliot's "The Social Function of Poetry," they also regenerate hegemonic culture.[5] In this way, *The Waste Land* suggests that one possibility for regeneration lies in the very act of literary interpretation.

Where, then, does Lil fit into the above scheme — into a historical and cultural context that *The Waste Land* suggests is sterile and into a deconstruction of and search for meaning-making structures? Furthermore, why might we even consider that she, rather than the mythological Tiresias or the meaning-making reader, is the "most important personage" in the poem? Our answer, as I suggested earlier, lies in the simple but inescapable facts of biology and, perhaps of gender.[6] As we journey through the landscape of *The Waste Land* we are not only encouraged to dismantle the meaning-making structures noted above; we are also urged to deconstruct the notion of a strong ruling and present father. In fact, the poem directly and indirectly suggests the absence of a regenerative male personage: "the king my father . . .," is dead, Phlebas the Phoenician is a "fortnight dead . . ."; "Hieronymo's mad againe . . ."; Tiresias — the presumably unifying personage of the poem — has undergone a sexual transformation; Mr. Eugenides "the one-eyed merchant, seller of currants" is homosexual; "The Hanged Man" cannot be found; Albert is absent; and, finally, in the spirit of Joyce's "Nighttown" episode in *Ulysses*, God has been linguistically transformed into a "Dog. . . ."

At the same time that it marks the absence of a strong male figure, *The Waste Land*, and particularly "A Game of Chess" and "The Fire Sermon," foregrounds a female iconography and offers a masculinist-modernist version of the image of the female. This sex-defined pattern of images supports the modernist illusion that the poets of the twentieth century, and in particular Eliot, were engaged in a project that would "make it new." We might argue that, within the context of this high-modernist project, a female dominated image pattern points to an intent to dismantle the patriarchy and to create, instead, new social hierarchies. In fact, Carolyn Heilbrun argues a closely related point in a discussion of Eliot's Tiresias — a figure that she claims to be a modernist representation of the androgynous ideal and thus a representation of a concept of sexuality that transcends and therefore redefines conventional notions of both sexuality and gender.[7]

Nevertheless, although the female-dominated image pattern of *The Waste Land* encourages interpretations that resemble Heilbrun's in spirit, interpretations that succeed in transforming the old into the "new," we must ask what the poem does, in fact, suggest we should conclude about modern culture and, more specifically, about psychosexual dynamics. To do so, we might briefly compare the conclusions suggested by Eliot's project with those suggested by Joyce's *Ulysses*. Like *The Waste Land*, the latter text questions conventional meaning-making structures, marks the absence of a strong father, and dismantles what Stuart Gilbert refers to as the "fiction of paternity."[8] Similarly, like Eliot's long poem, Joyce's novel accomplishes the former goals within the context of a structure that breaks with conventional notions of narrative, that thus makes literature appear "new" and that therefore may suggest a transformation of culture. But finally, in its so doing or undoing, *Ulysses* re-asserts conventional assumptions about the sexual hierarchies within modernist culture: the sonless Bloom reunites with the fatherless Stephen and in the end patriarchy, although itself slightly transformed, is strongly reasserted. In a similar way, and as Freud's *Civilization and its Discontents* and Bloom's *The Anxiety of Influence* suggest is inevitable, while *The Waste Land* appears to mourn the loss of male-dominated culture, seems to even intend to destroy the rule of the father — seems, that is, to actually intend to "make it new" — this surface appearance conceals yet a deeper wish — the wish to reinstate and reestablish the patriarchy that was originally destroyed.[9] Thus, as Terry Eagleton so rightly notes, *The Waste Land* reasserts the domination of male hegemonic culture, but does so under the guise of cultural collapse and disintegration.[10]

In addition to suggesting the ideological implications described above, the male/female pattern of images that emerges during our reading of *The Waste Land* has meaning in relation to the actual biological role that women have had and continue to have in culture and history (patriarchal and otherwise) and in relation to *real* questions concerning the continuation of civilization. As Dorothy Dinnerstein points out, despite the fact that women have been excluded from public history, that history has been and continues to be dependent upon women — at least, but not only, in so far as women are the procreative sex, the sex especially responsible for the continuation of the human species.[11] In so far as Dinnerstein is correct and women are biologically destined to bear children and in so far as *The*

Waste Land is concerned with the sterility of the land and its people, with the problems of regeneration, and with the effects of the former situation upon the continuity of patriarchial culture, it makes good sense that the long poem foregrounds the female image. It makes good sense, that is, because women — the childbearers — are directly responsible for the regeneration of the species and for the possibilities of cultural continuity.

Ironically, but in line both with Eliot's post-war concern with the sterility of a land and its people and with his modernist male anxiety about the biolgical powers of women, none of *The Waste Land* women bear children — none of the women, that is, save Lil. Lil, the working class woman with rotting and missing teeth is fertile. She can create new life, and she has done so. Within this frame, then, Lil holds the biological powers necessary to the continuity of history and culture. Therefore, I would suggest that she and not Tiresias is the "most important personage" in Eliot's long poem.

Our post-modernist revision of *The Waste Land* suggests both a reexamination of the mythologies that surround Tiresias and a recreation of Eliot's Lil. Therefore, we might next reconsider Eliot's "old man with wrinkled female breasts. ..." "... old man with wrinkled dugs. ..." Or, more precisely, we might reexamine the *fictions* that surround this modernist representative of the intermediate sex. Certainly, as post-modern post-new critical theory leads us to conclude, none of those fictions — regardless of their contexts — are embedded in the text.[12] Rather, they are readers' verbal fabrications. As such they are presumably generated from the dialectic between readers' mental structures; their inter-relationships with language, culture, and history; and their methods and processes of literary interpretation, on the one hand; and the units of the text, on the other. But in the case of the fictions that surround Tiresias, this dialectical process does not necessarily occur. Many of the typical fictions that surround Eliot's Tiresias — those that claim the mythological personage is the poem's "most important personage" and its unifying consciousness — are neither supported by the text itself nor by Valerie Eliot's recently published edition of *The Waste Land* drafts.

If my claim is correct and the typical Tiresian fictions that readers generate neither originate from nor are supported by the actual *The*

Waste Land text (i.e. the text minus its notes) how, then, do we account for the origin and popularity of those fictions? The answer is simple. As is well known, Eliot encourages readers to elevate Tiresias to the status of the "most important personage in the poem" and to imagine Tiresias as the unifying consciousness of *The Waste Land* in the concluding "Notes." Eliot writes:

Tiresias, although a mere spectator and not indeed a 'character', is yet the most important personage in the poem uniting all the rest. Just as the one-eyed merchant, seller of currants, melts into the Phoenician Sailor, and the latter is not wholly distinct from Ferdinand Prince of Naples, so all the women are one woman, and the two sexes meet in Tiresias. What Tiresias *sees*, in fact, is the substance of the poem. . . .[13]

Literary history indicates that as they weave their fictions about Tiresias many critics simply follow the recommendations of Eliot's "Notes." Many appropriate the poet's language. Some repeat; others slightly alter; and yet others extend his analysis. But what is striking is that most critics of *The Waste Land* preserve Eliot's basic assumptions about Tiresias and, as a consequence, about male-defined history and culture.[14]

Since many of the fictions that surround Eliot's Tiresias arise from *The Waste Land* "Notes," we might take a closer look at the *function* of those "Notes" themselves. On one level, innumerable critics have praised those notes for functioning as accurate keys to the complexities of both the meaning and structure of *The Waste Land*. Implicitly these critics, for example, G.R. Williamson, Elizabeth Drew, and Cleanth Brooks, valorize allusion hunts and the search for intertextual links; and they valorize a meaning-making process that results from the mental juxtaposition of texts and from the imagining of various semantic similarities and differences suggested by that very act of juxtaposition. Following the recommendations of Eliot's notes many critics also name Tiresias the consciousness that frames the entire poem and they transform him into a principle that gives structure to what seems to be an otherwise disunified text. In fact many of those critics who claim the mimetic veracity of *The Waste Land* extend this notion even further. Still following the recommendations of Eliot's notes, critics assume that *The Waste Land* is framed by an all-inclusive mythic perspective, that of Tiresias, and claim that because

Tiresias functions to unite "*all* the rest" (italics mine) *The Waste Land* is a universal text or, to quote from Gertrude Patterson, a text that embraces "the whole of society for all time. . . ."[15]

On the other hand, although popular among Eliot critics, the above view of *The Waste Land* "Notes" has not gone unquestioned, and rightly so. In a 1956 American lecture "Frontiers of Criticism," Eliot points out that the original "Notes" to *The Waste Land* were designed both to protect the poet against critics' accusations of plagiarism and to satisfy publishers' demands for a longer poem. In that same published lecture, Eliot refers to the "Notes" as a "remarkable exposition of bogus scholarship," and he declares that they "stimulated the wrong kind of interest among the seekers of sources. . . ." Finally, Eliot apologizes for "having sent so many enquirers off on a wild goose chase after Tarot cards and the Holy Grail."[16] With this perspective in mind, critics such as Hugh Kenner encourage readers to disregard *The Waste Land* notes and, instead, to engage the dialectic between mind and poem.

Nevertheless, while critics have viewed *The Waste Land* "Notes" as if they are mysterious keys to some sealed Pandora's box and as if they are misleading and to be discarded, none have yet spoken to the essential ways in which these "Notes" function as a device of literary repression; nor have they spoken to the ways in which these "Notes" function as one of the texts many misogynist strategies. For example, critics have not spoken to the way in which the note to Tiresias functions to conceal the anxiety-provoking dynamics of the structure of *The Waste Land*; the way in which it functions as a defense against the "anxiety of reading."[17] In essence, that note conceals the fact that the long poem's units of discourse are spoken by different speakers, many of whom remain unnamed and unnameable while nothing in the text itself functions to help us clarify the relationship between those units or voices or to help us synthesize those speakers. That note conceals the fact that nothing in the poem itself helps us to order its chaos or to make its parts cohere into a modernist "whole." In a more general way, that note functions to disguise the fact that our reading of *The Waste Land* requires us to confront the modernist anxiety about form, order, and unity and to search for a logical principle or a metaphor or paradigm with which to make sense of *The Waste Land*.[18]

Secondly as a repressive device, the reference to Tiresias in Eliot's "Notes" encourages us to focus our attentions upon that representation of the intermediate sex, to consider Tiresias to be the poem's unifying principle "uniting all the rest," and, perhaps, to consider Tiresias not only to be at the mathematical center of *The Waste Land* but to represent the poem's dramatic center: "Tiresias ... is yet the most important personage in the poem...." However, critics have not pointed out that while Eliot's *The Waste Land* note overtly leads us towards conclusions of this kind, it simultaneously defines the parameters of the meaning-making process and restricts it. In particular, that note deflects our attention from the importance of female biology and its role in history, in culture, and in the process of rejuvinating a wasted land. In effect, then, that note functions as one of a series of misogynist strategies — semantic and structural strategies that encourage readers to imagine women as paltry beings who are not only imprisoned in what Sherry Ortner refers to as a universally subordinated sub-culture, but who also deserve to belong to such a sub-culture — a series I will delineate further in the following section of this essay.[19]

Implicit allusions — allusions that are not marked by references in the notes to *The Waste Land* — are among the text's other misogynist strategies. As readers, we know that the allusions of *The Waste Land* urge us to link the long poem with the texts of Eliot's predecessors. But not only do allusions urge readers to link *The Waste Land* with those precursor texts; like other of the strategies of *The Waste Land*, allusions encourage readers to create deprecating and debasing stories about the women referred to in Eliot's long poem. So, for instance, Lil who is an anomaly in *The Waste Land* because she is a wife and mother is not unique in history. Rather, her image recurs. And although it recurs in slightly different forms, what is common among those forms is that they represent male fantasies about female possibilities and function as defenses against male anxiety about female sexuality and power. Thus, while they allow Eliot to contain his "fathers," such allusions also encourage tales about women that serve patriarchal culture.[20]

While Eliot clearly relied upon "the tradition" to support his construction of a literary framework that encourages readers to debase and degrade the female form, his own "individual talent" also furthered this political act of the imagination. Helen Vendler comments upon the nature of that talent in an essay entitled "T.S. Eliot." Vendler commends Eliot for the linguistic and stylistic authenticity of the pub scene. According to Vendler, Eliot "listened to what his maid said ...," wrote "it down ...," and made those words into "poetry."[21] In addition, Eliot added to the authenticity of that scene by situating it in a pub, by repeating the ritualistic "HURRY UP PLEASE IT'S TIME," and by including details that suggest stereotype working-class attitudes, behaviors, and economic concerns. As a result of these stylistic and linguistic devices, the pub scene gives us the illusion that what we are reading is a typical scene of working-class life and one that is presented from a neutral or, perhaps, Tiresian or mythological perspective.

What Vendler does not point out is that because the poetic surface of the pub scene itself seems to be authentic and because it suggests an authentic scene of working class life, it functions cosmetically and conceals the text's implicit ideology. Thus, on the surface, Lil's brilliantly sketched portrait may seem to suggest the image of a typical working-class woman, of a working class woman as she actually is. But although suggesting the illusion of mimetic verisimilitude, the diction and style of the pub scene conceal a deeper fact, the fact that the pub scene reinforces a perspective on women that is aligned with male versions of history and culture and that encourages readers to view Lil through the patriarchal structures of their own "immasculated" imaginations.[22]

In the case of the pub scene, Eliot further disguises the bias of the text by presenting the scene from the point of view of one of the pub "ladies." And yet, although a woman tells Lil's story, or the framework of that story, she neither creates that story from a "female" perspective nor from a perspective that is supportive of Lil. Nor is that story told from a neutral perspective. Rather, the text's sympathies lie with Albert and with masculine versions of history and culture. This point is suggested by the unnamed speaker's explicit reference to "poor Albert," a reference that suggests empathy with Albert's class status and, most importantly, with Albert's sexual needs rather than with Lil's unfortunate and complex circumstance. This implicit betrayal of Lil, a kind of female betrayal that Dorothy Dinnerstein claims to be necessary to the social and political domination of the patriarchy, is also highlighted by the monologist's attitudes towards Lil's unsightly appearance and her self-inflicted abortion.[23] In the former case, the speaker recommends that Lil make herself "a bit smart" and "get" herself "some teeth." We might expect these seemingly concerned comments to be motivated by care for Lil's health or physical well-being. However, we find that the unnamed speaker is concerned with whether or not the returned Albert will be pleased with and satisfied by his wife's appearance, a concern that even dominates the question of whether or not Lil wants to or will be able to keep her man:

> When Lil's husband got demobbed, I said—
> I didn't mince up my words, I said to her myself,
> HURRY UP PLEASE IT'S TIME
> Now Albert's coming back, make yourself a bit smart.
> He'll want to know what you done with that money he gave you
> To get yourself some teeth. He did, I was there.
> You have them all out, Lil, and get a nice set,
> He said, I swear, I can't bear to look at you.
> And no more can't I, I said, and think of poor Albert,
> He's been in the army four years, he wants a good time,
> And if you don't give it him, there's others will, I said.
> Oh is there, she said. Something o'that, I said.
> Then I'll know who to thank, she said, and give me a straight look.

Similarly, the passage's speaker questions Lil's abortion and calls her a "proper fool" not because the act is detrimental to Lil but rather because that bringing of "if off" violates unwritten historical and cultural rules regarding women's functions — rules, as I suggested earlier, that require women to donate their biology to a history that inevitably intends to exclude them. Thus, the speaker of the pub scene declares "What you get married for if you don't want children?"

In the end, Eliot's metonymic and mutilating references to Lil's rotting and missing teeth, her unbearable appearance, her "long face," her "antique" look, and her violent bringing of "it off," references that are framed by the perspective of a male-aligned female consciousness and presented in an authentic style, suggest the tale of a deteriorating, helpless, fragmented, self-destructive, and even,

perhaps, daemonic female. In effect, if we follow the recommendations of Eliot's text — strategies that I think defend the poet against a
modernist anxiety about female sexuality and power — then Lil
seems to be but a decaying body — an "empty chapel, only the wind's
home. . . ." In this way, and as Annette Kolodny's analysis of the traditional association of women and the land would lead us to conclude,
Lil is Eliot's wasted land.[24]

Conversely, while the image of the female Lil functions as a
metaphor for Eliot's wasted land, the image of "the waste land" that
appears in the title of Eliot's long poem, the image of a decaying,
desolate, spiritless land, functions as a metaphor for this modern
poet's more general attitudes towards women. Thus, the misogynist
strategies of Eliot's long poem suggest a legend of Lil that is yet
another version of the stories we are urged to construct about "the
typist" and the three Thames Maidens of "The Fire Sermon." Like
Lil, these latter fallen angels represent a masulinist-modernist intent
to violate women, to mutilate the female form, and to deny women
their spiritual and emotional freedom. Similarly, Lil's legend is also a
version of the tales *The Waste Land* urges us to create about the Sybil of
the long poem's epigraph and Madame Sosostris, "the famous clair-
voyante" who appears in "The Burial of the Dead." Unlike Lil,
neither of Eliot's muted interpreters are seen in relation to men.
However, the misogynist strategies of *The Waste Land* encourage
readers to strip the Sybil and Madame Sosostris of their powers of
interpretation and of their female voices; thus, like Lil, Eliot's muted
interpreters are rendered speechless and helpless. Finally, the tale of
the mutilated and mutilating Lil that is implicit in *The Waste Land* is a
version of the legends of the "hyacinth girl" and the "lady of situations" that the text also implies. Representing twentieth-century
revisions of the tradition's *femme fatale*, both the "hyacinth girl" and
"the lady of situations" are sexually alluring female types. Like Lil,
both of Eliot's fallen Cleopatras are bound to unfulfilling relationships
with men, trapped in misogynist interpretations of their own stories,
and imprisoned in a male-defined poetic space.

Rather than concluding with the above legends about the paradigmatic Lil and about her female *Waste Land* companions, I wish to
conclude by reminding us that the stories of Lil and of the other *Waste*

Land women we recreate are not only the products of these females' class status, their status as women, and the poetic strategies of both Eliot's long poem and the literary tradition. In addition, these fictions are also a product of readers' mental structures and imaginations. In effect, we read *The Waste Land* and with some prodding from Eliot, the tradition that he continues, and the unnamed speaker of the pub scene we generate our own literary fantasies, wishes, and desires and thus recreate a version of Lil's story. The tale of mutilation, dependency, fragmentation, and powerlessness referred to above is not only generated in response to Eliot's text and the tradition but is also created from the patriarchal structures and modes of interpretation embedded in readers' own psyches. Thus, in order to revise our legends of Lil and of the other women of *The Waste Land* and in order to reimagine Eliot's long poem, we can literally transform the text or we can activate and generate new structures of interpretation. The former is not a possible act. However, by activating alternative structures of interpretation we can discover another Lil or other Lils who wait behind the misogynist strategies of Eliot's text and yearn to be born. I am suggesting, therefore, that we turn away from the image of femaleness that "the tradition" and Eliot's "individual talent" seem to direct us towards and intend us to reimagine. In addition, I am suggesting that we look behind the misogynist strategies of *The Waste Land* and of tradition, strategies that stimulate and guide our recreation of Lil and her legends. Furthermore, we must deflect our attentions away from the images of wife and mother that history, literature, and the media overtly and covertly implant in our imaginations. And, as we turn away from these typical structures of interpretation, we must simultaneously begin to construct or rely upon new structures. For a start, let me suggest that we focus upon the power implicit in Lil's tale; thus, we can recover both that power and the perspective of a female imagination.

As I suggested earlier, Lil's power appears to be of the kind that is conventionally associated with women — that is, the power of procreation. As we know, Lil is married and, most importantly, she can and does bear children. But what we did not note earlier is that the power of Lil's biology is not the only power suggested by her female image. In addition, Lil represents a non-conventional and, perhaps, culturally threatening power. To clarify this point, we might consider Lil in relation to Lilith — a female imaged in Jewish lore:

Created not from Adam's rib but, like him, from the dust, Lilith was Adam's first wife, according to apocryphal Jewish lore. Because she considered herself to be his equal, she objected to lying beneath him, so that when he tried to force her submission, she became enraged and, speaking the Ineffable Name, flew away to the edge of the Red Sea to reside with demons. Threatened by God's angelic emissaries, told that she must return or daily lose a hundred of her demon children to death, Lilith preferred punishment to patriarchal marriage, and she took her revenge against both God and Adam by injuring babies — especially male babies, who were traditionally thought to be more vulnerable to her attacks.[25]

Lil, an aborted and aborting Lilith, also refuses to engage in the pre-defined identity that masculinist history offers to her, her foremothers, and her foresisters and that that history encourages women to participate in. So, in a way that is finally self-defeating because it leads to her own ill-health and to the continuation rather than the dissolution of her own entrapment, but in a way that represents the one viable alternative available to her, Lil, like Lilith declares "I prefer not to."

In such a context, Lil's mutilated appearance and her self-inflicted abortion acquire new meaning. Certainly, Lil's refusal to get herself "some teeth" and to take care of her physical appearance continue to be self-destructive acts. But they are now also more than or other than that. Now, Lil's appearance and behavior represent rebellious acts, acts that indicate her silent statement that she refuses to continue to participate in patriarchal definitions of attractive or appropriate female behavior. Similarly, Lil's self-inflicted abortion of her sixth child points to her refusal to continue to be a servant to a history that prohibits her from telling her own story and that finally intends to exclude and subordinate her. Rather than continuing to participate in that history, Lil takes power and control over her own body and biology. Unfortunately, she does so in a way that ultimately keeps her trapped. But although Lil may be a "proper fool," as the text's unnamed speaker declares, she is a rebellious rather than a submissive one.

Finally, as Dorothy Dinnerstein's analysis of psycho-sexual dynamics and of culture suggests may be inevitable, the power and willfulness of Lil, like that of Lilith, is contained by patriarchy and by its fantasies about the positions women are to hold in society.[26] Sandra Gilbert and Susan Gubar describe Lilith's situation as follows:

What Lilith's history suggests is that in patriarchal culture, female speech and female "presumption" — that is, angry revolt against male domination — are inextricably linked and inevitably daemonic. Excluded from the human community, even from the semi-divine communal chronicles of the Bible, the figure of Lilith represents the price women have been told they must pay for attempting to define themselves. And it is a terrible price: cursed both because she is a character who 'got away' and because she dared to usurp the essentially literary authority implied by the act of naming, Lilith is locked into a vengeance (child killing) which can only bring her more suffering (the killing of her own children). And even the nature of her one-woman revolution emphasizes her helplessness and her isolation, for her protest takes the form of a refusal and a departure, a flight of escape rather than an active rebellion like, say, Satan's.[27]

With some slight revisions, Gilbert and Gubar's words can also be applied to Eliot's Lil. What links the Biblical Lilith and the modern Lil is both women's wish to get away, the power they assert to realize that wish, and the vengeance and personal suffering to which that wish, stifled by the patriarchy, finally leads them. In effect, a complex network of male hegemonic defenses work against the female sexuality and power that women such as Lilith and Lil represent — women whose legends have been concealed, repressed, fragmented, revised, and silenced by a masculinist tradition.

Notes

1. The present essay is part of a longer study of *The Waste Land* that is now in progress: *The Anxiety of Reading: Portraits of the Women in The Waste Land.*
2. See, for example, James E. Miller, Jr., *T.S. Eliot's Personal Waste Land*, (University Park: The Pennsylvania State University Press, 1977), p. 8. Miller both confirms my claim that *The Waste Land* has been viewed as a poem about the sterility of a land and its people and he challenges that claim. Note that I am not claiming, as Miller suggests many critics have done, that *The Waste Land* is about the sterility of "the modern world." Rather, I am claiming that it is about the sterility of a world, what I believe to be a world of Eliot's own making.
3. See Terry Eagleton, *Criticism and Ideology*, Verso ed. (1975; rpt. Great Britain: NLB, 1978), p. 148-149. Eagleton points out that *The Waste Land* creates the illusion that hegemonic culture is disintegrating but that, in fact, the poem actually transcends that illusion and displays "an ideology of cultural knowledge."

4. Homosexual sex is not necessarily among the *conventional* meaning-making structures. However, it is among the structures that *The Waste Land* urges readers to deconstruct.

5. T.S. Eliot, "The Social Function of Poetry," in *On Poetry and Poets*, pp. 9-12.

6. For an account of the relationship between biology and gender see Dorothy Dinnerstein, *The Mermaid and the Minotaur* (New York: Harper & Row, Publishers, 1976), pp. 7-8.

7. See Carolyn Heilbrun, *Toward a Recognition of Androgyny*, (New York: Alfred A. Knopf, 1973), p. 11.

8. Stuart Gilbert, *James Joyce's Ulysses* 2nd ed. (1930; rpt. New York: Vintage Books, 1958), p. 59.

9. For a relevant discussion of Freud's *Civilization and its Discontents* see Dorothy Dinnerstein, pp. 181-184.

10. See Eagleton, pp. 148-150.

11. See Dinnerstein, pp. 20-21.

12. See, for example, Wolfgang Iser, *The Act of Reading* (Baltimore: The Johns Hopkins University Press, 1978).

13. T.S. Eliot, "Notes on 'The Waste Land'," in *T.S. Eliot The Complete Poems and Plays*, 11th ed. (1934; rpt. New York: Harcourt, Brace and World, Inc., 1971), p. 52. Quotations from Eliot's *The Waste Land* will refer to the above edition of the poet's work.

14. See Elizabeth Drew, *T.S. Eliot: The Design of His Poetry* (New York: Charles Scribner's Sons, 1949), p. 67. Grover Smith, *T.S. Eliot's Poetry and Plays*, 6th ed. (1950; rpt. Chicago: The University of Chicago Press, 1965), pp. 67-68. J. Hillis Miller, *Poets of Reality*, 2nd ed. (1965; rpt. Cambridge, Massachusetts: The Belknap Press of Harvard University Press, 1966), p. 174. Gertrude Patterson, *T.S. Eliot: poems in the making* (New York: Barnes & Noble Inc., 1971), p. 134.

15. The claim to the universality of *The Waste Land* has been suggested, for example, by Elizabeth Drew. See Drew, *T.S. Eliot: The Design of His Poetry*, p. 58.

16. T.S. Eliot, "The Frontiers of Criticism," in *On Poetry and Poets*, 9th ed. (1961; rpt. New York; The Noonday Press, 1970) p. 121.

17. The term "the anxiety of reading" has its origins in Bloom's "the anxiety of influence" and in Sandra Gilbert and Susan Gubar's "the anxiety of authorship." See Harold Bloom, *The Anxiety of Influence* (New York: Oxford University Press, 1973), p. 11. Also see Sandra Gilbert and Susan Gubar, *The Madwoman in the Attic*, 2nd ed. (1979; rpt. New Haven: Yale University Press, 1980), pp. 48-49. Rather than referring to the writer's creative anxieties, as my precursors' terms do, my term refers to the reader's anxieties — i.e. to the anxieties readers experience in the process of interpreting the text. I use the term in a most general way in the current article. However, I intend it most specifically to refer to readers' fears to pronounce non-patriarchal interpretations of literary texts.

18. For examples of the types of metaphors used to make sense of the structure of *The Waste Land* see, among others, Aiken, Frank, and Langbaum referred to above.

19. Sherry Ortner, "Is Female to Male as Nature Is to Culture?" in *Woman, Culture, and Society*, ed. Michelle Zimbalist Rosaldo and Louise Lamphere (Stanford: Stanford University Press, 1974), p. 67.

20. Christopher Ricks describes allusion as a device that allows a "son" to contain his "father". See Christopher Ricks, "Allusion; Poet as Heir," in *Studies in the*

Eighteenth Century III, eds. R.F. Brissenden and J.C. Eade (Australia: Australian National University Press, 1976), p. 231.

21. Helen Vendler, "T.S. Eliot," in *Part of Nature, Part of Us* (Cambridge, Massachusetts: Harvard University Press, 1980), p. 78.

22. I wish to thank Judith Fetterly for suggesting the term "immasculating imagination" to me. See Judith Fetterly, *The Resisting Reader: A Feminist Approach to American Fiction* (Bloomington: Indiana University Press, 1978), p. xxvi.

23. Dinnerstein, pp. 46, 51.

24. Annette Kolodny, *The Lay of the Land* (Chapel Hill: The University of North Carolina Press, 1975), p. 6.

25. Gilbert and Gubar, *The Madwoman in the Attic*, p. 35.

26. Dinnerstein, p. 202.

27. Gilbert and Gubar, p. 35.

A struggle for survival: Edith Summers Kelley's *Weeds*

BARBARA LOOTENS

English Department, Purdue University North Central

ALTHOUGH I HAD read Tillie Olsen's *Silences* and accepted her definition of the literary canon which consciously or unconsciously conspires against novels written by women, a full understanding of the silences imposed upon women writers and, therefore, upon their readers came from my experience with *Weeds*, a moving and powerful story of life in the tobacco-growing hills of Kentucky during the period surrounding World War I. Written by Edith Summers Kelley (1884-1956), it was first published in 1923 and reprinted in 1972 and 1974 to introduce the series Lost American Fiction (Southern Illinois University Press). In 1976 I was forced to borrow a copy from my daughter, who had borrowed it from a friend; but by 1978, when I attempted to use the book in a course on women novelists, it was already out of print. With the exception of single copies in libraries and a rare find on a used-paperback shelf, the book itself seemed to have vanished — even though its title occasionally popped up like a ghost on lists of books written by women.

In 1981 during the NEH Summer Seminar "Feminism, Modernism, and Feminist Criticism," directed by Sandra Gilbert and Susan Gubar, I compared notes with my fellow participants and unearthed stories similar to mine. No one had been able to use *Weeds* as a text. In spite of the enthusiastic response from everyone who had read it, *Weeds* seemed threatened with extinction, a fate unbelievable in light of highly favorable reviews fifty years apart. It was with a sense of elation

Women's Studies, 1986
Vol. 13, pp. 103-113
0049-7878/86/1302-0103 $18.50/0

that a few weeks after the end of the seminar I received notice of the decision by The Feminist Press to reissue *Weeds* in January, 1982. Now that the novel is available, the question still remains of whether, by itself, another reprinting can have the power to break Edith Summers Kelley's tragic silence.

Joseph Wood Krutch, reviewing the novel in 1924, may have unknowingly anticipated one reason for its failure for over half a century:

A play must come to a definite conclusion but the essence of the tragedy of life is that life does not. When a hero is stabbed in the back and the stage is strewn with bodies, things at least have come to an end and we are cleanly done with them, but in life we must live on though the interminable *irrelevance* (italics mine) of the sixth act and the most painful part is the anti-climax which must be endured (*Nation*, January 16, 1924).

It may be that Kelley's unsentimental, undramatic portrayal of Judith Pippinger Blackford's life is too painful and despairing to have captured the imagination of the general public, for in spite of the efforts of influential friends (among them Upton Sinclair and Sinclair Lewis, who as late as 1941 tried to get the novel reissued as a book club selection), Edith Summers Kelley remains "an obscure and sad figure" in literary history (Matthew Bruccoli's Afterword in the 1972 edition). (The additional biographical facts provided by Charlotte Goodman in the new edition only heighten this observation.)

One explanation for the failure of the novel in the 1920's could be that it simply reached the wrong audience, one not ready or willing to see in themselves the tragic vision which was so readily accepted in the next decade (i.e., *The Grapes of Wrath*), and certainly its realistic method would not have appealed to the avant-garde literary establishment. By the time the novel was re-issued in the early '70's, Kelley's purpose could have seemed to run counter to the political climate of the feminist movement which tended either to de-emphasize feminine roles in both life and literature or to favor those examples which emphasized oppression imposed upon women by the patriarchal system.

Whatever the reasons for the book's failure in the past, I agree with The Feminist Press that *Weeds* is a major work which should not be permitted to die from neglect or misunderstanding. Yet the question persists of whether this novel will be able to reach a wide enough audience to guarantee its survival. Even if it were to gain admission to the tradition of the "divided stream" of American naturalism, as Charlotte Goodman suggests in her Afterword, the likelihood of its catching the attention of the general public is remote as long as the book is confined to academia, where it is viewed as a work to be "studied." Somehow, millions of women outside the university need to be made aware of a novel which speaks directly to them with compassion and truth — a feat difficult to accomplish without the attention of critics published in popular periodicals. This is where feminist readers can make the difference. Through their thoughtful reading and discussion of the novel, both inside and outside feminist circles, they may be able to provoke the desire to make *Weeds* accessible to the public.

Speaking to and of those women unable to articulate their own lives, Kelley answers to a need which has rarely been met in contemporary fiction. Without condescension and with a sureness derived from her own experience, she presents a view of womanhood which must be recognized. For millions of women there simply are not and may never be the options so confidently explored in many recent novels. Circumscribed by poverty, tradition, and biological demands, millions of women must confront the reality of lives little different from those of their mothers and grandmothers. To these women, Edith Kelley speaks with compassion and understanding. For those of us able to assume some power over our own lives, Kelley makes real a world that most of us have chosen not to know.

Although I agree completely that Krutch's "interminable sixth act" is essential to an understanding of Kelley's *Weeds*, I do not accept his conclusion that the novel is basically the story of Judy Blackford's "disappointment in life" or her "descent from the eagerness of youth to the acquiescence of age" — nor do I completely agree with Matthew Bruccoli's conclusion that Kelley's protagonist bows to her fate with "passive acceptance." To reach only those conclusions is to trivialize Kelley's work. On the other hand, I do not want to suggest that Kelley's intention in any way contributes to the "Schlaflyesque" vision of the glory of woman fulfilling her proper role. In fact, the surface details of *Weeds* would suggest just the opposite — that motherhood, which is implicit in the image of woman, is the symbol of degradation. The real strength of Kelley lies in her success in mediating these two views of motherhood by embedding within a seemingly straight-forward narrative the pattern of Sophoclean tragedy.

In this sober and painful work Kelley's protagonist, "larger than life," "a poppy among weeds," is, like her ancient counterparts, caught in a trap not entirely of her own making. In spite of her faith in her own ability to evade the fate which is prophesied by those around her, Judith Pippinger Blackford falls victim to the very forces which she feels will sustain her. Yet, like her literary ancestors, she emerges — if not in triumph — at least with self-knowledge, making it possible for her to assume the power which comes from that understanding. In a paradoxical way, Judith's defeat is transformed to an affirmation of womanhood, and, therefore, of the human condition, tragic as it is.

After setting up her rebellious heroine who, like Oedipus, refuses to accept the role defined by the generation before her, Kelley in a chorus-like passage presents the human consequences of the divine plan: "As soon as one generation was laid low another came to take its place. The earth teemed with the seed of this useless but vigorous and persistent life" (p. 213). More specifically, while tracing Judy's life through childhood, marriage and motherhood, Kelley carefully creates the savage and harsh world to which Judy belongs. "Ironically, Judy's people exhaust their bodies and their spirits in a vain effort to make a living from a weed, tobacco. As they battle against weeds to grow weeds, an analogy between the endless, senseless cycle of nature and the cycle of human life becomes plain" (Coppélia Kahn, *Ms.*, April, 1974).

Bill Pippinger foreshadows not only his daughter's tragedy but the vigor with which she struggles against the forces threatening to destroy her when he proudly proclaims, "Land, that little gal's got life enough for a dozen sech — too much life, too much life for a gal" (p. 14).

Although nature will trap her as it had the women who preceded her, in Judy's girlhood it appears that "somehow in spite of her ancestry, she had escaped the curse of the soil, else she could never have known to be so free, so glad, so joyous" (p. 88). Unaware of the insidious shadows which will darken her life, Judy watches with no more than childish curiosity when for her mother's funeral the women of the neighborhood dye black the little red dress her mother had made for her. It is not that she remains unaware of the cruelties of nature and the blight which destroys all living things; rather, spending most of her time out-of-doors, she outgrows the initial horror and grief she feels when kittens die, flowers wilt, and one animal is destroyed by another, for something instinctive within her knows that "in the life of nature death and suffering are merely incidentals, that the message that nature gives to her children is 'Live, grow, be happy and obey my promptings'"(p. 22).

In her unity of body and spirit, "not much more given to thinking than was the mocking bird in the hickory tree over the house" (p. 140), Judy stands apart from others of her sex. "Almost all of them, daughters and mothers alike, were painfully thin, with pinched angular features and peculiarly dead expressionless eyes. The faces of the girls already wore an old, patient look, as though a black dress and a few gray hairs would make them sisters instead of daughters of older women" (p. 85). In contrast, "Judith in red and white (shines) in her dark loveliness like a poppy among weeds" (p. 88). She attracts the attention of Jerry Blackford, who later seeks her out under the pretext of looking for his red and white heifer. Spontaneously and naturally, Judy obeys nature's promptings, thereby falling into nature's trap.

With the exuberance of a young animal, she begins her marriage, heedless of the prophetic words of Kelley's Tiresias figure, Jabez Moorhouse. "The young Toms'll be cut off in the pride of their lives and the turkey hens'll live to raise up families an' the families they raise'll repeat the same thing all over again an' so on world without end. Amen" (p. 68).

Together Judy and Jerry work in the field, exulting in their love and in their hopes for the future. Although exhausted at the end of long days spent topping tobacco plants, fighting tobacco worms, and feeling that "her row would never come to an end" (p. 139), when Judy lies beside Jerry, she feels that "there was something restful and satis-fying about the firm enfolding male pressure. Her hand, lying in his, felt relaxed and at peace, like a child rocked by its mother" (p. 101). Suddenly afflicted with a disease "shrouded in mystery," Judy recoils when her neighbour Hat Woolf, with a kind of malicious glee, en-lightens her about her pregnancy. She protests, "But, Hat, a caow

ain't sick when she's a-fixin to have a calf!'" (p. 147). After Hat's rejoin-
der that "wimmin has troubles caows don't never even dream on,"
Judy retreats to "the clean earth to shake from herself the close and
foetid atmosphere of Hat's hollow" (p. 148). However, she cannot
escape from the older women who speak to her of her pregnancy with
intimacy and secrecy as if she had now joined their "vile and disgust-
ing" company, where "prying old eyes" leer from gloomy corners (p.
157). She learns to lock the door and hide in the bedroom whenever
she sees a female figure approaching the cabin, trying to evade the
chorus of women whose own lives warn her of her fate. When the
symptoms of early pregnancy subside, she rejoins Jerry in the fields,
delighting in her freedom and rejoicing in the sense of new birth,
"overflowing with physical well-being and spiritual content" (p. 149).
In spite of the brutal labor, as she works in the fields, Judy is happy out
of doors, secure in her belief that the sun means "joyous life and
growth" (p. 140). By contrast, "she had always disliked the inside of
houses. The gloom of little-windowed rooms, the dead chill or the
heavy heat as the fires smouldered or blazed, the prim, set look of
tables and cupboards that always stood in the same places engaged in
the never ending occupation of collecting dust both above and
beneath: these things stifled and depressed her. She was always glad
to escape into the open where there was light, life, and motion and the
sun and the wind kept things clean" (p. 116).

As Judy's tragedy unfolds, she will see taken from her all of the
things which give her joy. In an incantation reminiscent of Tiresias'
doleful prophecy to Oedipus, Kelley forecasts Judy's fate:

Families must be fed after some fashion or other and dishes washed three times a day,
three hundred and sixty-five days in the year. Babies must be fed and washed and
dressed and 'changed' and rocked when they cried and watched and kept out of
mischief and danger. The endless wrangles among older children must be arbitrated
in some way or other, if only by cuffing the ears of both contestants; and the equally
endless complaints stilled by threats, promises, whatever lies a harassed mother could
invent to quiet the fretful clamor of discontented childhood. Fires must be lighted and
kept going as long as needed for cooking, no matter how great the heat. Cows must be
milked and cream skimmed and butter churned. Hens must be fed and eggs gathered
and the filth shoveled out of henhouses. Diapers must be washed, and grimy little
drawers and rompers and stiff overalls and sweaty work shirts and grease-bespattered
dresses and kitchen aprons and filthy, sour-smelling towels and socks stinking with
the putridity of unwashed feet and all the other articles that go to make up a farm

woman's family wash. Floors must be swept and scrubbed and stoves cleaned and a never ending war waged against the constant encroaches of dust, grease, stable manure, flies, spiders, rats, mice, ants, and all the other breeders of filth that are continually at work in country households (p. 195).

Throughout the novel Kelley plays upon the symbols of light and dark so much a part of Sophoclean tragedy and, like her predecessor, she uses them to create a correspondence between the natural world and her protagonist's spiritual condition. In addition, Kelley provides a particularly feminine touch with the repeated use of color, especially the colors of dresses which reveal the inward as well as the outward state of her character. In a springtime escape from the house and her first child, Judy goes to town with Jerry wearing a white dress with tiny red dots and a sunbonnet made from a red bandana. She buys bright calico for the baby's dresses and cannot resist a white muslin with pink rosebuds for herself. In Judy's choice of the pink flowers is reflected her unconscious knowledge of the fading of her own beauty, in the white muslin the dissipation of her own vitality. The sturdy, bright calico for the baby suggests the price that motherhood will exact.

The sun, too, reverses its meaning for Judy. Drought comes and with it a sun which sears the soil, kills the new growth, and destroys the labor of months. Jerry, with no work to do in the fields, helps Judy with the laundry at a nearly dried-up spring in the hollow. As the baby crawls through the "wild weed jungle" grasping with "his helpless chubby hands at butterflies and flecks of sunlight," Judy, pregnant again, withdraws from Jerry and wishes that she could crawl into a hole "like a wild creature of the woods" (p. 189). Feeling "as bleak, dry, desolate, and soulless as the landscape," she yearns for "a hole where there were no meals to cook, no fire to keep going, no fretful child to pacify — a nice dark, quiet hole where nobody ever came and where she could curl up and be at peace" (pp. 207-08).

Like all classical protagonists, as Judy becomes more and more embroiled in the endless struggle against her fate, she rebels more and more passionately and more and more futilely. With heroic rage she flails out at those around her, becoming totally estranged from Jerry, hating his dog-like devotion, his cheerfulness, even his acts of kindness toward her. When the child's demands become too persistent, she slaps him savagely, feeling that both he and the unborn child are vampires sucking away her blood and her life. She begins to hate Jerry and his masculine vitality, of which she feels herself the victim; yet even more she hates herself, yearning to be a willing victim like her sister Lizzie May, who is content to dye rags bright colors and keep her house clean like a tame rabbit that shuts itself into a cage and spends its time working to keep the cage clean. Although she knows that she loves her children, would die for them, she also knows that she begrudges them something. Trapped in the house, unable to work in the fields or roam freely in the hills as she used to do, Judy alternatively resists and submits to her maternal bondage, the monotony broken only by Jerry's accounts of his days and by occasional 'visits' where she clutches eagerly at "those tattered scraps of other people's lives" (p. 160).

As in classical tragedy, where the hero, caught in the whirlpool of his own agony, is unable to realize any tragedy but his own, so Judy, isolated in her own anguish, recoils from Jerry and the children (now three). After desperate and unsuccessful attempts to save herself by re-establishing her harmonious ties with nature, she makes an abortive attempt to recapture her lost sensuality with an itinerant evangelist. In a scene drawn from the convention of the choral song and dance, Kelley too gives her protagonist a brief reprieve. On her way to meet her lover Judy is shocked to discover a red, not pink, rosebud on a stunted, distorted bush outside the house. 'Inhaling the fragrance and looking into the deep richness of the scarlet leaves, she felt carried beyond herself with great uplifting of heart. Tears from some strange hidden source welled into her eyes" (p. 273). In the disillusionment of the love affair which she knows was bred of desperation, Judy sees that "after its one rose had shed its leaves, the little bush, discouraged by the drought and the continual pecking of the hens, had dried up and leveled itself with the ground" (p. 273).

Just as the ancient gods continue to heap insult after insult upon their already-vanquished victim, so Nature continues its assault upon Judy. As if something meant to punish her for her refusal to concede to Nature's power or to prove to her once again her subservience, Judy finds herself pregnant. Unable to bear the thought of another unwanted child, she retreats to the woods in a wild ride on a mule, hoping to induce an abortion. Caught in the pleasure of the animal's speed, she experiences for a moment the glory and freedom of movement she had known as a child. In an attempt to transcend her own flesh, she fantasizes that she is God looking at "poor children he had made in his own image and condemned to a life of toilsome grubbing in the dirt. . . . (p. 285). But like all heroic figures, Judy is not able to blind herself. "She faced the abysmal truth that she was not God, but only one of these pitiful, groveling creatures doomed to the same existence and the same end" (p. 285). With this self-knowledge, Judy longs, like Oedipus, for death. Unable to face a life without hope, she attempts to drown herself in the horse pond. But her ties to the earth are too strong. Her own nature will not let her die. And, like that of Oedipus, her own nature forces her to look outside herself, to recognize her complicity in a tragedy more encompassing than her own personal one. No longer with revulsion but with cosmic sorrow, she sees the faces of her children and knows that their fate is bound up with her own. In her sons she sees "traces of the look she had learned to dread, a look that stamps itself upon the faces of these who for generations have tilled the soil in solitude, a heavy, settled unexpectant look" (p. 279). But it is because of her daughter Annie that the pain engulfs her. Puny, colorless, with "blank slate-colored eyes" (p. 280), she lies in her cradle making delicate cooing sounds "sweet as flower petals" (p. 281). Judy recognizes this child, "this one that had come out of her own body . . . In every way, she was a product of the life that had brought her into being, and that life would claim her to the end" (p. 321).

As Judy suffers with her daughter during an illness, she questions why the child should live, why this child should be "another strong added link to the sodden life of the soil" (p. 322). Just as painfully, she experiences shock and heartbreak when she realizes that Jerry, somehow without her noticing, is turning into an old man, eating and drinking bestially, lurching in weariness with heavy and dragging steps. When she agrees with his often-repeated words of comfort, "Don't worry, Judy, as long as you and me's got each other, things'll be all right," she hides her face, for she knows she's lying.

At the moment of her defeat, however, Judy Blackford discovers that even though she is tied to the earth and must eventually submit to its power, she is tied by stronger bonds to her children and her husband for as long as she lives. Although a part of the natural process, she cannot bow to nature by retreating animal-like to a dark hole nor can she abandon herself to the mindless and useless howling of an animal caught in a trap. As a human being, she must deny these instincts, must assume the human prerogative to act in accordance to human needs. Somehow she must find the courage to move out of the darkness to the lighted cabin where Jerry and the children, hungry as wolf-cubs, are waiting for her. Judy has no illusions about the meaning of her life. She accepts the future as "a sad, dead level of unrelieved monotony," knowing "she would go on all her allotted time bearing and nursing babies and rearing them as best she could. And when her time was over, she would go back to the field, like other women, and set tobacco and worm and top tobacco, shuck corn and plant potatoes. Already people were beginning to call her Aunt Judy. Some day she would be too old to work in the field and would sit all day in the kitchen in winter and on the porch in summer shelling beans or stripping corn on the cob. She would be grandmammy then" (p. 331).

With the full knowledge given to great and heroic figures, then, Judy Blackford assumes the power to endure with dignity. Although doomed to spiritual isolation, she alone can provide the strength for her family. "Together there would be if not happiness at least peace and a measure of mutual comfort and sustaining strength by virtue of which they might with some calm and self-respect support the joint burden of their lives" (p. 331).

It is this understanding and the dignity with which Judy Blackford confronts her fate that gives *Weeds* the power of a truly great tragedy. And for women of the 1980's Edith Kelley provides important insights which transcend perceptions about the fate of one simple girl in a primitive, poverty-stricken landscape. Whatever their public and private roles, all women must recognize that, despite the tragedy underlying the human condition, female strength can create human bonds, based upon the human values of dignity and self-respect, perhaps the only catharsis possible in modern society and one for which Edith Summers Kelley deserves full artistic recognition. For feminists, the implications of including Kelley's view of womanhood in the literary canon go far beyond the vindication of one woman writer. The first step in the destruction of the myth of the artistic irrelevance of an ordinary woman's life, acceptance of *Weeds* is acceptance of the right of women to establish new literary traditions evolving from essential female experience.

Avoiding self-definition: In defense of women's right to merge (Julia Kristeva and *Mrs Dalloway*)

JEAN WYATT

Occidental College, Los Angeles

IN MANY twentieth-century novels by women the protagonists, and, one assumes, their authors, too, affirm a sense of self in flux, traversed by changing currents of feeling and spreading beyond Western culture's definition of a contained ego to merge with what is outside. The female characters don't rush to define what is inchoate and amorphous in themselves, but welcome the chaos of a diffuse self for its promise of change and celebrate the possibilities for renewal in the experience of merging. Often, as in *The Awakening, Mrs Dalloway, The Waterfall, Surfacing,* and *Housekeeping,* water or ocean images signal the character's immersion in life processes beyond the individual. Using Julia Kristeva's theories together with examples from Virginia Woolf's *Mrs Dalloway,* I will argue here that a return to an undifferentiated state of being is not merely regressive, as Freudian developmental charts based on male patterns of growth would have us think: viewed in a context of female experience, the capacity for opening up to identification and fusion reveals revolutionary and renewing powers.

In *Civilization and Its Discontents* Freud describes the diffuse and undefined state that is our original sense of being as the "oceanic" feeling. (*Mrs Dalloway,* I hasten to add, described becoming one with the world in ocean images four years before the publication of the first chapter of *Civilization and Its Discontents* in 1929.)

Women's Studies, 1986
Vol. 13, pp. 115-126
0049-7878/86/1302-0115 $18.50/0

An infant at the breast does not as yet distinguish his ego from the external world. . . . originally the ego includes everything, later it separates off an external world from itself. Our present ego-feeling is, therefore, only a shrunken residue of a much more inclusive — indeed, an all-embracing — feeling which corresponded to a more intimate bond between the ego and the world about it. If we may assume that there are many people in whose mental life this primary ego-feeling has persisted to a greater or less degree, it would exist in them side by side with the narrower and more sharply demarcated ego-feeling of maturity, like a kind of counterpart to it. In that case, the ideational contents appropriate to it would be precisely those of limitlessness and of a bond with the universe — the "oceanic" feeling.[1]

Notice that Freud does not make value judgments on the two ways of being he describes here: they exist as alternative states of mind in the same individual, available to him/her throughout life. But in other texts Freud made the oral (merging) stage the first in a series of psychosexual stages. In the hands of Freud's followers his description of growth becomes prescriptive, and earlier stages are dismissed as primitive. Cynthia Griffin Wolff, for example, takes Edna, the protagonist of Chopin's *The Awakening*, to task for her desire to fuse with the world around her:

A psychologically mature individual has to some extent satisfied these oral desires for limitless fusion with the external world; presumably his sense of oneness with a nurturing figure has given him sustenance sufficient to move onward to more complex satisfactions . . . Edna's hidden self longs for resuscitation and nourishment. . . . It is an orally destructive self, a limitless void whose needs can be filled, finally, only by total fusion with the outside world, a totality of sensuous enfolding. And this totality means annihilation of the ego.[2]

Wolff assumes that a firm ego, set off from the surrounding world, and connection limited to a genital relationship, are the prizes of maturity, the only adult kinds of being and relating. Freud's description of development has been frozen into steps up a marble staircase that must be taken in order, and only for the purpose of getting to the top, "a genuine genital relationship."[3]

Norman Holland, who follows Freud's developmental scheme, too, in constructing a "Dictionary of Fantasy," similarly implies that the desire to fuse with one's surroundings is primitive and must encounter a healthier impulse, the desire for separation. "The single most common fantasy-structure in literature is phallic assertiveness balanced against oral engulfment."[4] Taking over the male paradigm of development from Freud, Holland assumes fusing is the loss of self (engulfment), so that it must call up a defense of autonomy in the symbolic form of the phallus (characteristically, Holland overlooks the plight of those without one). The male literary examples of merging Holland chooses to cite, such as Poe's stories of being buried alive or devoured, are tinged with terror. What is remarkable about fantasies of merging in women's fiction, however, is that fusion seems desirable, indeed natural: characters in women's novels seem to feel as if they had regained their natural state rather than losing it; in place of fear and frantic defense, female characters experience joy and fullness of being.

Carol Gilligan has pointed out that most developmental theories — Freud's, Erikson's, Kohlberg's — are based on men's interpretations of data drawn predominantly or exclusively from studies of male subjects. These theories assume that the stages of male development are the norm and fault women when they depart from them. Gilligan suggests that what fails is not women, but the theory that measures them. More specifically, girls' persistence in defining themselves in relationship has been considered a failure in individuation.

The quality of embeddedness in social interaction and personal relationships that characterizes women's lives in contrast to men's ... becomes not only a descriptive difference but also a developmental liability when the milestones of childhood and adolescent development in the psychological literature are markers of increasing separation. Women's failure to separate then becomes by definition a failure to develop.[5]

Nancy Chodorow, in her encyclopaedic compilation and interpretation of psychoanalytic theory on mothers and daughters, *The Reproduction of Mothering*, demonstrates that because of the institution of exclusive mothering girls follow a different developmental track from boys. In the nuclear family structure that psychoanalytic theory assumes as the basis of early childhood experience — in which childcare is the principal job of the mother — all infants go through stages of primary identification and symbiosis, when mother and infant feel fused. After these early stages, mothers tend to perceive their sons as male others, reinforcing their efforts to differentiate. But they unconsciously define their daughters as extensions of themselves. The confusion of "you" and "me" shows up in projections of their own feelings and needs onto their daughters and overinvestment in areas that are properly their daughters' own — bodily functions such as eating, for example. Girls have corresponding problems recognizing themselves as separate from their mothers; issues of individuation and differentiation are not confined to the first stages of childhood, as the developmental charts say they should be, but extend into adolescence. Even as young adults, even as they function in the world as autonomous beings who cognitively recognize their separateness, "most girls . . . in relation to their mothers . . . experience themselves as overly attached, unindividuated, and without boundaries."[6]

The effects of growing up with a definition of self in relationship are both positive and negative. The cases reported by Jean Baker Miller of autonomous women successful in their own right who feel their experience is meaningless without a man to witness it demonstrate the crippling effect of feeling one is nothing outside relationship.[7] But women are also more skilled at empathy, more capable of feeling — or believing they feel — what others feel. And because girls "fuse the experience of attachment with the process of identity formation,"[8] because they feel continuous with their first environment longer than boys, they can more easily transcend the limiting boundaries of the isolated self to feel at one with the world.[9]

To be sure, there are exceptions to this gender-specific model: witness male religious mystics and, among male writers, Proust, who establishes a sense of identity laboriously, and always in relation to his immediate environment; but then Proust, as much as any female child, felt fused to his mother — indeed, to his whole maternal line — so that he experienced his mother's absence as a loss of self. In psychoanalytic theory's description of normative male development, though, the addition of erotically tinged oedipal love to the boy's primary identification with his mother makes her such a toweringly powerful figure that she seems to threaten his separate existence altogether;[10] in order to separate from her and identify with men, always more distant than the ever-present mother, the boy cuts himself off sharply from his mother and — a deformity that Chodorow blames on the institution of exclusive mothering — from his own internalized maternal qualities of tenderness and desire for intimacy. Although Holland presents his examples of literary fusion as universal, they are marked male by the threatening presence of "an all-powerful, maternal woman" and the fear of engulfment.[11]

Of course, girls also feel ambivalent about merging with an all too close mother.[12] But one may theorize, with many twentieth-century novels bearing out the theory, that women are more comfortable vaulting over ego boundaries to fuse with what is outside than are men because what Freud calls the "oceanic feeling" is built into their primary definition of self; they are more apt to experience expansion into the environment as a "bath of blisse"[13] than as drowning.

Carol Gilligan's argument encourages us to look at old definitions of what is valuable in human development from new perspectives grounded in women's experience rather than borrowed from male models. I wish to confront Wolff's and Holland's Freudian assumptions about what progress means in human development with Julia Kristeva's theories of change. Change is more chaotic and continual in Kristeva's theory than in Freud's model of measured progress through a fixed succession of stages. Kristeva thinks of the mature human being as embodying a dialectic between the semiotic self and the symbolic self — more process than progress. She neither disparages the diffuse sense of self and the urge to merge associated with infantile oral drives nor endorses a sharply defined ego as the goal of human development. Rather, drawing on Jacques Lacan's rereading of Freud, she presents the coherent ego as an artifice, constructed first on the model of the alienated image the infant sees in its mirror reflection, then on the representation of the self in the field of language. Both models are distinct from the real, corporeal experience of the child. As the mirror image is a mirage, so is the notion of a self-contained ego based on it. Similarly, "I" is not a product of my shifting experience of sensations and feelings, but a construction imposed on that inchoate reality by the communication system's need for a unitary source of speech. "I" leaves out everything particular to me, reduces me to an abstract term, the same for everyone. "I identify myself in language, but only by losing myself in it like an object," says Lacan.[14] Kristeva maintains that "the subject is merely the subject of predication, of judgment, of the sentence."[15] I create myself as an independent entity by forming a sentence around the subject "I"; "I" am therefore in continuous production, generated by my statements. When "I" establish my position as subject, I differentiate myself from the objects I talk about: speech generates not only "I," the speaker, but "them," the objects that language requires I treat as separate from myself. The "symbolic" self, then, is a momentary position in the field of language. But "a symbolic system corresponds to a specific structuration of the speaking subject within the symbolic order."[16] Since the social and language systems that construct the symbolic self insist on the fixity of their categories, the symbolic self is also rigidly defined and compartmentalized and reflects the pretense to permanence of the social institutions in which it is embedded.

Such a symbolic self-construct leaves out the "semiotic," a mode of being rooted in infancy, less a distinct entity than an undifferentiated field across which the instincts play. Kristeva picks up Freud's emphasis on the contradictory nature of the primary impulses that govern the semiotic: the urge to assimilate what is good in the environment, the urge to expel what frustrates, causes tension.[17] The heterogeneity of the instincts destroys any stasis: what characterizes the semiotic self is fluidity, produced by drives that change constantly both in nature and in aim.[18] Although when the child enters language s/he must give up the open-ended, diffuse self for the fixed position of speaker, the semiotic continues to circulate beneath language, disrupting from time to time the symbolic identity of the speaker. The ever-changing intensities of the body's impulses explode the illusion of a static circumscribed ego, leaving us for a time just a field for fluctuating impulses — until the need to represent ourselves in the social field of language requires the reformulation of a unified symbol for the self.[19] Unlike Wolff and Holland, then, Kristeva celebrates the resurgence of oral instincts because they destroy and cause the transformation of a seemingly static social identity, throwing social systems that rest on the unity of the individual citizen into question, too.

Mrs Dalloway implies that alone, without the social scaffolding of discourse, we are diffuse, not just internally — subject to the changing currents of impulse and feeling — but externally as well: without firm boundaries, the self merges with its surroundings. Clarissa on her morning walk through London loses her separate identity to

> the ebb and flow of things . . . [she was] part of the trees at home; of the house there . . . part of people she knew best, who lifted her on their branches as she had seen the trees lift the mist, but it spread ever so far, her life, herself.[20]

Joy floods her as the ocean image signals her expansion beyond ego boundaries to merge with the world. When she is forced into separation, defining herself "against" the June morning rather than immersed in it, despair robs her of life:

> she stood alone, a single figure against . . . the stare of this . . . June morning . . . feeling herself suddenly shrivelled, aged, breastless, the grinding, blowing, flowering of the day out of doors, out of the window, out of her body and brain which now failed.[21]

Far from fearing the loss of self in merging that Holland cites in male fictions of fusion — a fear which apparently accompanies the sense that the ego must be clearly defined and defended — Clarissa loses life when she can't merge.

In solitude, Clarissa's consciousness resembles Kristeva's definition of the semiotic self, an amorphous field coursed by the succeeding intensities of primitive drives: the urge to incorporate beloved surroundings, the desire to expel what produces internal tension (here, the image of Clarissa's hatred, Miss Kilman, an internalized monster who "grubs at the roots" of Clarissa's soul).[22] Although I agree with Phyllis Rose that "there is no way fully to explain or analyze the lift of the spirit that occurs when one reads certain parts of *Mrs Dalloway*,"[23] I hazard the guess that we willingly overlook Clarissa's classbound superficialities, her snobbism, her overinvestment in social success and failure, because the novel hits us not at the level of our social selves, but at the level of our primitive oral impulses: in Clarissa's blissful merging we experience our own desire to escape encasement in a circumscribed ego, to reinstitute our original boundless sense of a self merged with the world; and in her despair at the loss of connection we feel again the pain of our original separation from the enfolding world — cast out, alone, into an alien universe.

The rhythms of the ocean surge through the passages describing the loss of clear distinction between the self and the world, calling up in the reader a semiotic level of self.

Quiet descended on her, calm, content, as her needle, drawing the silk smoothly to its gentle pause, collected the green folds together and attached them, very lightly, to the belt. So on a summer's day waves collect, overbalance, and fall; collect and fall; and the whole world seems to be saying "that is all" more and more ponderously, until even the heart in the body which lies in the sun on the beach says too, That is all. Fear no more, says the heart. Fear no more, says the heart, committing its burden to some sea, which sighs collectively for all sorrows, and renews, begins, collects, lets fall. And the body alone listens to the passing bee; the wave breaking; the dog barking, far away barking and barking.[24]

Prose becomes incantation, working on the reader's susceptibility to rhythm; it imitates the ocean's repetitions in persuading the reader, too, to give up the burden of the structured symbolic self who decodes abstract words for the sensual self who lets the words' rhythms play across her/his body as the regularity of the waves' breaking plays on the body that lies in the sun on the beach.

According to Kristeva, a text can precipitate a takeover by the semiotic in the reader.[25] When the rhythmic patterns become the organizing principle of a text, edging out grammatical order, words begin to strike the reader as sounds rather than conveyors of meaning. We respond to words as we did in infancy, when we registered the sound, rhythm, music of words rather than their significance. The position of detached analytic reader structured by the conventions of the realistic text disappears, and we become semiotic, responding to words with what is left out of the socialized "I": fluctuating instinctual responses. Since this state of being has its source in a period of time when we did not distinguish ourselves from our environment, semiotic language also recalls a self without firm ego boundaries. The reader is thus encouraged to imitate the dissolution of Clarissa's social self into a rhythmical space played on by oceanic patterns of alliteration and repetition.

If a female reader is more accustomed to lose the distinction between herself and her surroundings as a result of her prolonged lack of differentiation from her first maternal environment, does she respond more readily to this appeal to give up the separate detached self and merge with the rhythms of the novel than a male reader does? Is she quicker to surrender the detached self of the analytic reader and dissolve into the flux of sensations called up by such an appeal to the semiotic level of her experience? The psychoanalytic picture of female development as formulated by thinkers like Gilligan and Chodorow suggests that she might be more comfortable with a personality in flux, more able to shift to a diffuse reader who is simply a sequence of responses.[26]

Kristeva conceives the self as process: the semiotic self, a succession of intensities originating in the drives, must make way for the symbolic self which we are all obliged to consolidate into a single shape in order to represent ourselves to others; but drive energy overwhelms and shatters the unitary self, causing a reformulation. Clarissa similarly moves from being a receptacle for fluctuating intensities — joy, love, hate, fear — to a socially defined unitary personality. But while the fluctuating, unbounded self of her morning walk comes naturally and fills her with vitality, she must labor to create a unified ego:

> collecting the whole of her at one point (as she looked into the glass), seeing the delicate pink face of the woman who was that very night to give a party; of Clarissa Dalloway; of herself. . . . She pursed her lips when she looked in the glass. It was to give her face point. That was her self — pointed; dartlike; definite. That was her self when some effort, some call on her to be her self, drew the parts together, she alone knew how different, how incompatible and composed so for the world only into one centre, one diamond, one woman who sat in her drawing-room and made a meeting-point, a radiancy no doubt in some dull lives, a refuge for the lonely to come to, perhaps.[27]

Woolf anticipates Lacan in her choice of props for Clarissa's moment of self-definition: the mirror, which returns a unified if alienated image ("the delicate pink face of the woman"); her name, indisputably singular; her role as hostess ("the woman who was that very night to give a party"); and the self-contained image of her that others see ("one woman who sat in her drawing-room and made a meeting-point"). The discrete entity "herself" is not an intuitive certainty, but a laborious reconstruction of her "point" in the network of family names and social roles. Society requires that people be circumscribed individuals so they can play the singular parts designed for them by social systems. As Linda Mizejewski points out in a perceptive Whiteheadian analysis of *Mrs Dalloway*, it is "for the world only" that Clarissa feels compelled to gather herself together, "because the world cannot comprehend the multiple, contradictory, expanded selves, events and processes we really are."[28] The clearly demarcated self-contained ego is a construct, Woolf implies: Clarissa needs all the resources of naming and placing that social systems can provide to force the heterogeneous facets of her self to one point in the social network, one "diamond," artificially dazzling but inorganic in contrast to the living mobility of Clarissa's consciousness.

Juxtaposing Kristeva's theories with Woolf's novel gives rise to questions rather than leading to conclusions. Do we operate in two widely different modalities in solitude and in dialogue? If the structured social self is a product of speech and social intercourse, does it disappear when we cease speaking? Without the social scaffolding of conversation, do we lose structure and become fluid, a succession of feelings and intensities? If so, is the self in solitude the authentic one, multiple, diverse, fluctuating, while the coherent ego is fundamentally an illusion, a social artifice constructed by language systems? Do men and women have fundamentally different conceptions of themselves based on differences in their primary experience with their mothers? Is the model of a clearly demarcated separate ego a male paradigm of individuality based on the male child's need to cut himself off sharply from continuity with an overwhelmingly powerful mother? Although Kristeva does not specify the gender of her model, is her notion of a self in process in fact closer to the way women perceive themselves?[29] Certainly her contemporaries, Hélène Cixous and Luce Irigaray, picture woman as diffuse and undefined, "a moving, limitlessly changing ensemble, a cosmos tirelessly traversed by Eros," in the words of Hélène Cixious.[30]

It is difficult to argue for Cixous' description of woman as permanently "undifferentiated, unbordered, unorganized ... incoherent, chaotic."[31] As Kristeva says, to remain in the semiotic mode, to be merely a flux of drive energy, would be to remain in "an underwater, undermaternal dive,"[32] unable to act or think effectively, a prey to violent impulses; what imparts vitality and change, Kristeva maintains, is the alternation of oral self and speaking subject. Dread of losing the self forever is implicit in the metaphors Holland uses to describe male literary fantasies of merging: "being engulfed, over-whelmed, drowned, devoured, or ... buried alive."[33] Indeed, Septimus' death in *Mrs Dalloway* by merging seems to confirm the fear that if one's identity is undefined and continuous with the environment, one disappears into it. I would like to propose a model like

Kristeva's: an "underwater dive" followed by emergence. Clarissa can merge with the "ebb and flow" of life in the London streets because her "little room" offers her the possibility of reconstituting self-containment. On the other hand, if Clarissa were self-enclosed all the time, on the model of the clearly demarcated ego at the top of Freudian developmental charts, she would not be open to the renewal and impetus for change that come from merging with different lives. Because she can identify completely with Septimus, because she can "lose herself" in the process of living — but "only to find it again"[34] — her self, porous and open to the lives of others, can absorb parts of their experience to expand in a way closed off to rigidly crystallized egos. She emerges from fusion with Septimus radiant with new vitality and expanded awareness. In *Mrs. Dalloway* and the twentieth-century women's fiction generally, merging sustains and expands the self rather than destroying it.

Notes

1. *Civilization and Its Discontents* (New York: Norton, 1961), pp. 13-15.
2. Cynthia Griffin Wolff, "Thanatos and Eros," rpt. in *The Awakening* (New York: Norton Critical Edition, 1976), pp. 210-11.
3. Wolff, p. 213.
4. *The Dynamics of Literary Response* (New York: Oxford Univ. Press, 1968), p. 43.
5. Carol Gilligan, *In a Different Voice* (Cambridge, MA: Harvard Univ. Press, 1982), pp. 8-9.
6. Nancy Chodorow, *The Reproduction of Mothering* (Berkeley: Univ. of California Press, 1978), p. 137. Marianne Hirsch has used Chodorow's description of the preoedipal phase to identify a developmental schema that distinguishes the female *Bildungsroman* from the normative structure of the male *Bildungsroman* in the nineteenth century: the heroine moves inward and back toward a spiritual reality characterized by preoedipal "fusion, fluidity, mutuality, continuity, and lack of differentiation." "Spiritual *Bildung*" in *The Voyage In*, ed. Elizabeth Abel, Marianne Hirsch, and Elizabeth Landland (Hanover and London: University Press of New England, 1983), 27. See also Hirsch's analysis of mother-daughter continuity in "A Mother's Discourse: Incorporation and Repetition in *La Princesse de Clèves*," in *Yale French Studies*, 62 (1981), 67-87; and her survey of the psychological literature of mother-daughter relations in "Mothers and Daughters: A Review Essay," *Signs* 7, 1 (Autumn 1981), 200-222.
7. *Toward a New Psychology of Women* (Boston: Beacon Press, 1976), pp. 83-85.
8. Gilligan, p. 8.
9. Chodorow, p. 103. Evelyn Fox Keller proposes a new, complex autonomy that includes some of the advantages of fluid ego boundaries in her model of "dynamic autonomy." *Reflections on Gender in Science* (New Haven and London: Yale University Press, 1985), 95-114.

10. Dorothy Dinnerstein vividly described the influence of exclusive mothering on men's perceptions of women in *The Mermaid and the Minotaur* (New York: Harper and Row, 1976).

11. Holland, p. 35.

12. Chodorow thinks girls turn to their fathers not so much because of the sexual issues Freud emphasizes as because an alliance with him is the only alternative available in the nuclear family structure to a dependent relationship with the mother (pp. 117-129).

13. Chaucer, *The Canterbury Tales*, "The Wife of Bath's Tale," in *Chaucer's Poetry*, ed. E.T. Donaldsen (New York: Ronald Press, 1975), p. 230. Cited by Holland, p. 35.

14. Jacques Lacan, *The Language of the Self*, tr. Anthony Wilden (Baltimore: Johns Hopkins, 1968), p. 63.

15. "From One Identity to Another," in *Desire in Language* ed. Roudiez (New York: Columbia Univ. Press, 1980), p. 130.

16. Julia Kristeva, *Pouvoirs de l'Horreur* (Paris: Editions du Seuil, 1980), p. 82.

17. Freud, "Negation," Standard Edition, ed. Strachey (London: Hogarth Press, 1973), pp. 235-239.

18. Kristeva, *La révolution du langage poétique* (Paris: Editions du Seuil, 1974), pp. 17-150. For a comprehensive explanation of Lacan's and Kristeva's theories, see Rosalind Coward and John Ellis, *Language and Materialism* (London: Routledge and Kegan Paul, 1977).

19. Kristeva gives a dramatic presentation of the dissolution and reformulation of her own identity in "The Novel as Polylogue" in *Desire in Language* (New York: Columbia Univ. Press, 1980), pp. 162-66.

20. Virginia Woolf, *Mrs Dalloway* (New York: Harcourt, Brace, 1925), p. 12.

21. Woolf, *Mrs Dalloway*, p. 45.

22. Woolf, *Mrs Dalloway*, p. 17.

23. *Woman of Letters: A Life of Virginia Woolf* (New York: Oxford Univ. Press, 1978), p. 128.

24. *Mrs Dalloway*, pp. 58-59.

25. Kristeva dramatizes, in "The Novel as Polylogue," the shattering effect of Phillipe Sollers' *H* on her symbolic self (in *Desire in Language*).

26. Judith Kegan Gardiner uses Chodorow's theories of female personality structure to explore similar issues of reader identification in "On Female Identity and Writing by Women," *Critical Inquiry* 8 (Winter, 1981), 352-358.

27. Woolf, *Mrs Dalloway*, pp. 54-55.

28. "Modernist Heresies: Virginia Woolf's *Mrs Dalloway*," paper presented on the panel "The Lost Brother," MLA Convention, December 1982, p. 7.

29. Linda Mizejewski, in the article cited above, and Valerie C. Saiving and Penelope Washbourne approach the issue of female identity as process from a Whitebreadian perspective: Saiving, "Androgynous Life: A Feminist Appropriation of Process Thought," and Washbourne, "The Dynamics of Female Experience: Process Models and Human Values," in *Feminism and Process Thought* (New York: Edwin Mellen, 1981).

30. "The Laugh of the Medusa," *Signs*, 1 (Summer 1976), 880.

31. "Castration or Decapitation?" *Signs*, 7 (Autumn 1981), 46.

32. Kristeva, "The Novel as Polylogue," in *Desire and Language*, p. 164.

33. Holland, p. 35.

34. Woolf, *Mrs Dalloway*, p. 282.

Portrait of an artist as a woman: H.D.'s Raymonde Ransom

MELODY M. ZAJDEL

Department of English, Montana State University

H.D. IS KNOWN primarily as a poet, but throughout her career she continually wrote fiction as well. In the five works published during her lifetime (*Palimpsest, Hedylus,* "Narthex," *Kora and Ka* and *Bid Me to Live*), H.D. experiments with a number of modernist techniques and modes, including stream-of-consciousness narration, montage structure, and the theme of the *Künstlerroman.* While the *Künstlerroman* is by no means an unfamiliar form among modernists, H.D. adds a new slant; through her female protagonists, H.D. particularizes the demands and difficulties involved in becoming a woman artist. One of her more developed portraits of the woman artist is Raymonde Ransom, a poet who writes under the androgynous pen name of Ray Bart. Raymonde is distinctive as H.D.'s only protagonist to appear twice, in *Palimpsest* (1926) and "Narthex" (1928). This double appearance within the relatively short span of two years focuses the reader's attention on her and provides not merely a sense of continuity, but of growth within the two stories.

Raymonde is a poet who clearly recognizes her talent, but is (or has been) tempted by historical circumstance and love relationships to minimize her own artistic gift. Through the course of the two stories, Raymonde reviews and reconsiders her past, resists false or gender-simplistic definitions of herself, recognizes the damaging dominant-submissive sex-typed relationships which Rachel Blau DuPlessis has termed "romantic thralldom,"[1] and resolves to move beyond them.

Women's Studies, 1986
Vol. 13, pp. 127-134
0049-7878/86/1302-0127 $18.50/0

The emotional and intellectual complexity of such a progression is not treated lightly by H.D.. Indeed, the complexity and subtlety of Raymonde Ransom's life closely mirrors that of H.D. herself during the decade of the 1920's. Thus, an investigation of Raymonde Ransom reveals an articulate statement by a major feminist modernist writer about the problems and powers inherent in becoming a modern woman writer.

Raymonde Ransom first appears in the "Murex: War and Post War London" segment of H.D.'s first novel, *Palimpsest.* "Murex" recounts an afternoon and evening in Raymonde Ransom's life in which she relives her past (through flashbacks and memory) and then transforms her changed understanding of that past into a work of art, a poem. The piece opens with Raymonde's meeting with a young actress, Ermy Solomon, whose artist-lover has been seduced by a mutual acquaintance, Mavis Landour. Ermy comes to talk to Raymonde, ostensibly to obtain letters of introduction, but really because ten years earlier Mavis had similarly betrayed Raymonde's friendship by appropriating her husband, Freddie. Raymonde, who on her trips to London was able to "blur her acute perceptions . . . be in a state of expectation . . . [a] twilight of the spirit,"[2] does not wish to see Ermy. She particularly does not wish to confront her own memories, which she has been successfully repressing. The meeting with Ermy forces Raymonde to concentrate on both the present (Ermy's loss of a lover) and the past (her own loss of Freddie). Woven into the hearing of Ermy's story is Raymonde's revision and revitalization of her own experiences: her relationship with Freddie, Mavis' betrayal, the birth of her stillborn daughter, even the war itself.

But if Ermy's visit revives the past, Raymonde's understanding is completed only by the transmission of these experiences into poetry, the metamorphosis of Raymonde Ransom to Ray Bart. Ray Bart has always known that art gives back the eternal pattern, the frozen moment of understanding: "Art was magic . . . Poetry was to remember" (PAL, 155). Able to see the configuration of relationships, Ray Bart can transform experience into verse, thereby rendering its significance. Appropriately, the completion of Ray Bart's poem at the end of the story signals the final understanding of Raymonde Ransom and the reader.

One of the compelling facts of the past that Raymonde comes to understand is the significance the World War had on her personally and aesthetically. The death of a generation of men, in particular her poet-husband Freddie, has left her alone, heir to the artistic future. Ray Bart, not her male contemporaries or any of her successors, is all that remains of the world that was shattered and buried with the men of her own generation. Freddie himself realizes this just before his death at Vimy, and expresses forcefully his realization when he is home on leave:

"Look here, Ray, there ain't no damned poets," the voice was going on. It was not Ermentrude certainly. It was a throaty voice with seriousness overlaid by eternal blitheness, by eternal light cynicism, by eternal wit and glamour of something — long ago, long ago. Keats, Shelley, Browning. "There ain't, I tell you none, and now darling Raymonde there won't be." "Won't Freddie, be?" I mean these very neat trenches with all modern conveniences are not con-*doo*cive to poetry." "Yes, Freddie. But — but — afterwards." "My dear precious and guileful and sweetly gullible, Ray Bart. There ain't (ain't I told you?) going to be no — afterwards." ... "Freddie, Freddie — there will be —" "What most optimistic transparent transpontine?" "Poets." "One — yes one — poet." "Freddie —" "No. Ray Bart."

(PAL, 135)

Thus, Ray Bart — the one poet — has to go on, must write, for she is the only one left to tell the story, to link the pre-War and post-War worlds, the only one left capable of forging her experience and perception with the eternal patterns which are the real world of the poet.

In the first half of "Murex," Raymonde comes to her understanding subconsciously, by her merging and emerging visual and aural images. Her subconscious understanding, which will lead to her acceptance of her role as poet (as well as indicate her method), starts when

There was a sound of feet. There were feet, feet, feet, feet passing up Sloane Street on the way to Victoria. London had forgotten. She was one with London. She had forgotten... Feet were passing on the way to Victoria. Carry on. Carry on. Carry on. She had forgotten feet, feet, feet, feet. .... Raymonde wasn't going to face the matter. If Mavis wanted the young man and if Mavis got the young man — All's fair in love and — feet, feet, feet, feet.

(PAL, 98-99)

The marching feet are the echo of the past, Raymonde's experience of

World War I in London where soldiers were constantly marching to the troop trains. Within a page, however, another association is added: her husband Freddie. Freddie is one of the feet, part of her repressed past:

Her [Ermy's] husband. O bother. Let her keep her husband out of it. Raymonde didn't want to hear anything whatever about Ermy's husband ... Raymonde wanted to shout at Ermy, "play the game. Shut up. Don't you see I am, everyone is always fighting, always fighting to — forget? Like London — to forget — feet — feet — feet — feet — feet? ... anything was better than talking about husbands and feet — feet — feet — feet — feet.

(PAL, 100)

Reliving the experience of lying in the hospital, in childbirth, Raymonde hears the marchers pass her window and relates them to her own labor and stillborn child.

Long ago. Far and far and far as far as a buried Egyptian's neatly painted coffin, as far even as 1917. It was settled then forever. It was settled then forever, Feet — feet — feet — feet — Or was it a heart beating? There seemed to be a succession of muffled tread-ings, of sliding, of slitherings even as she looked at Ermy.

(PAL, 110)

The associative power of "feet, feet, feet, feet" becomes even more merged with her labor, as the nurse tells her, "It will be much worse before it's any better" (PAL, 141). And "it" does get worse: Raymonde's daughter is stillborn while outside her window the war's slaughter continues. The sound of marching feet emerges in Raymond's consciousness as the image of the world shattered by war:

Everything's altered horribly. That was the crux of the whole dreary matter. Every-thing had so horribly altered and there were new ways of looking at things and Raymonde and her like were centuries apart (who of their generation wasn't) from the young people who weren't, all in all, so much younger than they were. Feet, feet, feet, feet, feet. There was no use going on. Everything in life was blighted, still-born — that was the crux of the matter. Feet, feet, feet, feet, feet. They were a still-born generation.

(PAL, 117)

The final transmutation of feet occurs when her associations of death, the war and Freddie pivot to Freddie, his still-born poetry, the pre-War past and her own poetic creations.

That pain and that sound and that rhythm of pain and that rhythm of departure were indissolubly wedded. Or was it her heart beating? Feet, feet, feet, feet. No, Freddie, no Freddie not metres. Not poems. Not that kind of feet, Not trochaic, iambic or whatever, no verse, free or otherwise. I am listening to something. To feet, feet, feet, but not that kind, not your kind Freddie. No not iambic feet, no beat and throb of metre, no Freddie. I don't want to write it.

(PAL, 145-146)

Despite her disclaimers, it is precisely this transfiguration which must take place. To deal with the pain and loss, she must turn to Freddie's feet, to poetry. All the other feet, all the other associations, will be fused into this new meaning. It is only the creation of Ray Bart's poem which allows Raymonde to confront her experience, to complete the cycle of her understanding.

Faces, people, London. People, faces, Greece. Greece, people faces. Egypt. James Joyce was right. On, on, on, on, and out of it like some deep-sea jewel pulled up in a net squirming with an enormous catch of variagated squirming tentacled and tendrilled memories, just this, this — *who fished the murex up?*

(PAL, 157-158)

Raymonde Ransom transforms herself into the murex-fisher, the poet, Ray Bart, for only in this form can she integrate her experience and her understanding of "The gem, the eternal truth, the eternal law, the song" (PAL, 158). Whatever her other options in the future, the role of poet is inescapable.

For Raymonde Ransom, the creation of poetry is understanding and responsibility all at once. At the end of "Murex," she is prepared to return to Cret d'y Vaud to write, recognizing that her solitary creative power is the most significant determinant of her character, past and present:

It was Cret d'y Vaud that was her inspiration. O Cret that would never answer. It was Cret d'y Vaud more distant, more remote than all the ghostly Freddies, yet static, eternal like the jacinth behind antiquity. Now she may say that I adore her face — the room eternally the same, and thousands of years and interspersing civilizations but the armchair the same and the note book and the pencil, implements of her trade.

(PAL, 169)

Raymonde Ransom's revitaled and revised past has yielded two important points to her awareness of her own identity: first, she is a real poet (the only one, perhaps) and that can neither be denied by others nor herself; second, her ability to create the poem releases her from a false romantic past which, in the form of London and Freddie, too frequently had blurred her perceptions and undermined her sense of accomplishment and self-worth.

Raymonde Ransom's second appearance in H.D.'s fiction, in "Narthex" (1928), expands on this portrait of an artist as a woman. As in "Murex," Raymonde Ransom here recognizes her ability as an artist and the responsibilities this implies. Since an artist is sensitive to a world of meaning which lies underneath reality as it is commonly seen, Ray Bart is an initiate in the use of hieroglyphs, "getting things (thoughts, sensation) across in some subtle way, too subtle to grasp with intellectual comprehension . . . Hieroglyph language had beat in her room in London. . . ."[3] Since the poet is the cultural means of giving form to these hieroglyphs, and since so few people seem to know this subtle reality, being an artist takes precedence over other roles.

But "Narthex" goes beyond this and recognizes the temptations for a woman such as Raymonde Ransom (*sans* her Ray Bart helmet) to renounce the role of artist for the role of lover, wife and mother. The woman artist, in this work, finds herself at odds with the cultural norm of self-effacing love. Alex Mordaunt, a Anglo-Indian soldier of her own generation, wants Raymonde to marry him and have children. As Raymonde recognizes " 'You ought to have two children' meant two things, actual realism of all life in its full emotional completion or actual destruction" (NAR, 231). But the demands of time and attention required by the role of wife and mother are seen, by Raymonde Ransom, to prohibit the role of artist. More and more during her London summer, Raymonde comes to see self-effacing love as directly, destructively opposed to her identity as an artist. The situation with Mordaunt is all the more ironic and detrimental because he, too, writes verses, verses which Raymonde recognizes as inferior to her own:

. . . "He thinks you'll marry him, coddle his pretentious little pseudo-literary ambitions." Wasn't that temptation? It's easier to lull the threadbare second-rate into smug contentment, lull oneself into self-effacement with it, than to compass fresh creation. Dope artistic consciousness out of all existence, bring carpet-slippers, mix a little night cap. Irony stalking blatant had enticed Raymonde, irony saying man, woman, you are woman, he is apparently man. Man-woman, a temptation. The intellect grows sterile being bisexual ... or a-sexual.

(NAR, 233)

Mordaunt tempts Raymonde with two things: first, a socially and sexually satisfying relationship, and second, the promise that if she married him, she could write better. "If you lived, you might really write ... something. Not this unwholesome introspection ..." (NAR, 233). Raymonde is seriously drawn to Mordaunt, almost hypnotically so, for he offers the material, human alternative to her poetic, inhuman life of the imagination. He appears to her "like the priest of some cult of which I am ignorant, so something certainly not to do with intellect" (NAR, 259). And this is, of course, extremely tempting.

But Raymonde acknowledges the flaw of this temptation: she sees that to accept the socially prescribed secondary role in this particular man-woman relationship is to deny herself as poet and, through her as instrument, poetry itself. As she tells Daniel (another London friend), "Men have a way (the world accepts) of sinking with women to their lowest. Now with a mind, a sort of blade beating itself raw in your raw forehead, a woman like myself must have some such anodyne" (NAR, 259). Mordaunt is her proffered anodyne, the acceptable alternative to her complaint of being tired of writing, tired of the demands it places on her. But she is unable to accept him — or more importantly, her self-negation when she is with him. Although it is ultimately her friend Gareth who tells her to leave London, to go back to d'y Vaud and her writing, Raymonde goes because of her own inability to devalue her worth as an individual and as an artist. Certainly, that is the realization implicit in her remembrance of her response to his poetry:

Heavy trampling of great hooves [one of Raymonde's images for Mordaunt] might trample out the thing in her that burned and burned ... but the thing in her that burned and burned became like glass spikes under the great hooves of Mordaunt ... and her desire to deceive him into thinking she could accept him became so great that she overdid it ... So anxious to make him think he was the more important that she leapt over, over the other side and instead of being trampled into numb obscurity (why won't the gods let one just be trampled?) spiking little acrid pin points into his weighty ankles. Give up, give in.

(NAR, 257-258)

But she can't give up. Undermining her desire to give in is Mordaunt himself. Mordaunt fails to see his own inadequacy as a writer and feels it possible, almost necessary, to reform Raymonde. Even when he has no real claim, other than his self-importance as a man, to correct her, Mordaunt acts out his prescribed gender role within their relationship: protector, judge, teacher, dominant personality. This is a turning point for Raymonde. As an artist, she morally cannot sanction the second-rate, or deny the first-rate, or, quite simply, marry Mordaunt.

For Raymonde Ransom, "Nathrex" brings the recognition that what she wants transcends the socially prescribed gender roles offered her. She emerges from the story determined to continue alone as a poet and to seek in her art an increased understanding of herself and the means of synthesizing the seemingly dichotomous roles of woman and artist in her life. H.D.'s Raymonde Ransom doesn't resolve all the tensions apparent to both herself and her creator. Still, she provides a clear view of one major feminist modernist's perception of woman as artist. Raymonde's life as presented in both "Murex" and "Narthex" delineates the conflicts for the woman artist which are, very specifically, gender related. In doing so, H.D. shows both the personal and social struggle inherent in the feminist *Künstlerroman.*

Notes

1.   Rachel Blau DePlessis, "Romantic Thralldom in H.D.," *Contemporary Literature,* 20, No. 2 (Spring 1979), 1978-2003.
2.   H.D., *Palimpsest* (Carbondale: Southern Illinois University Press, 1968), p. 95. Parenthetical page references in the text, preceded by PAL, will be to this edition.
3.   H.D., "Narthex," *The Second American Caravan,* eds. Alfred Kreymborg, Lewis Mumford and Paul Rosenfield. (New York: Macauley, 1928), pp. 256-57. Parenthetical page references in the text, preceded by NAR, will be to this edition.

Gender and the great war: The case of Faulkner and Porter

ANNE GOODWYN JONES

University of Florida, Gainesville

WITHIN WESTERN CULTURE, attitudes to gender and to war have long been linked. For men, war has meant a chance to confirm, or recreate, the traditional sense of manhood as courage and physical prowess, grace under pressure. With the men gone, war has meant a chance for women to act with unwonted independence and authority and thus to reshape traditional womanhood. But after wars end, though men sustain traditional manhood in peacetime, changes in women's traditional roles have not typically persisted. Carol Berkin and Clara Lovett point out that, despite the "remarkable fluidity of circumstances and the innovative quality" of wartime experience, traditional roles and structures are resilient, and egalitarian reform is fragile.[1]

The First World War seems to challenge Berkin and Lovett's thesis. Not only did trench warfare and long distance weapons explode the tradition of masculine war heroism, but — even more interesting — combat experience replicated for many men what had been largely female experience.[2] Eric Leed, for example, explains how evolving defense strategies forced soldiers to confront the absence of clear boundaries, of territorial integrity. Such an absence typifies female experience, according to Nancy Chodorow.[3] Other traditionally female experiences Leed describes include enforced passivity, entrapment within enclosed space, marginalization, and a rejection of hierarchy. Not only did soldiers undergo female experience; the

Women's Studies, 1986
Vol. 13, pp. 135-148
0049-7878/86/1302-0135 $18.50/0

widespread feeling that the fathers had sent their sons to be killed further challenged identification with the patriarchy. One might expect that such men would use their war experience not to confirm but to question the meaning of gender. (Although Leed studies only the experience of European men, American men imaginatively and to some extent literally shared that experience.) Indeed, some did begin to question traditional gender-definitions. But only for a while, as we will see with Faulkner.

Women's experience in World War I suggests that it too might prove the exception, that for these women, wartime liberation might last. Even in the United States, women worked in the peace and preparedness movements, in industry, in relief agencies, as nurses, as yeomen in the Navy.[4] Moreover, such expansions of traditional roles came at a time when the suffrage movement was in full force. And after the war came the apparent liberations of the Jazz Age. Yet after the war, in the United States, the percentage of women who worked outside the home returned to the prewar figure — 25% — and stayed there until 1940. Social norms generally continued, despite the flapper sensation, to prescribe "separate and segregated spheres of activities for men and women"; women's sphere remained "family, hearth, and home."[5] World War I may thus have been no exception at all, at least for Americans. The war fictions of southern modernists William Faulkner and Katherine Anne Porter can show us the struggle over gender, as it was triggered within the male and the female imagination by this war. Further, they suggest a way to understand the retreats — male and female — from gender redefinition.

Incurable fictionalists, both Faulkner and Porter changed their names and their pasts to create autobiographical personae. Those personae embedded their authors firmly within the traditional values of the southern patriarchal aristocracy.[6] Porter identified herself as "the grandchild of a lost War,"[7] just as Faulkner identified himself with his great-grandfather William Clark Falkner, the Old Colonel, a decorated hero of the Civil War. In other words, when the First World War began, both inevitably saw it through the lens of the Civil War. Recently devastated by Estelle Oldham's decision to marry another man, Faulkner enlisted (posing as an Englishman) in the RAF in Canada, apparently hoping either to die or to salvage his damaged sense of manhood in the European air battle. When he failed to get there and probably even to fly solo, he invented another persona, this time a wounded war hero, a fiction he sustained for much of his life. Porter had by the time of the war left her first husband and gone alone to Chicago, where she worked (when she could) as an actress, and eventually to Denver, where she held a job as a newspaper reporter. Though no one has yet confirmed the story, Porter claimed that in Denver she fell in love with a handsome soldier (as a Civil War belle might have done); he died during the 1918 flu epidemic after nursing her back to health.

But however firmly they chose to embed themselves personally in traditional southern notions of gender, both Porter and Faulkner used the war in their stories and novels to question those very traditions, Faulkner primarily interrogating the southern gentleman and Porter the southern lady. It is in these stories (set in and written during a period of roughly twenty-two years, from 1918 to 1940) that we can also trace the processes through which they closed off their investigations of gender, though they did so for very different reasons, and in very different moods.

As Richard Milum has recently observed, Faulkner was deeply involved in the southern myth of heroic manhood, the cavalier ideal.[8] According to that myth, the Civil War produced the South's *chevaliers*, cavalrymen who brought to war and to love the art of chivalry. Because success in battle and in love meant success as a man, war and gender were intimately linked. Faulkner articulates his yearning for this ideal in the depiction of Civil War hero Bayard Sartoris in *Flags in the Dust*,[9] a novel whose main action, set just after World War I, includes later Sartorises. The Civil War Bayard Sartoris, as one of Jeb Stuart's cavalrymen, rides with them right into the heart of a Union camp — in search of coffee, a romantic flip of the nose at the Yankees. When a captured Union officer later taunts Stuart, saying that in this war "gentlemen" of this sort are as anachronistic as "anchovies," Bayard turns around and rides back, this time for anchovies. He is shot in the back by a cook. Though Bayard dies before he can prove his manhood in chivalric love as well as war, Jeb Stuart suggests that role. For Aunt Jenny (who tells Bayard's story) ends her narration by saying, "'I danced a valse with [Jeb Stuart] in Baltimore in '58,' and her voice was proud and still as banners in the dust" (*FID*, 23).[10]

If the first Bayard Sartoris's story embodies the chivalric ideal, the story of the second Bayard, who fought in World War I, embodies its loss, as most commentators have agreed. Beyond *Flags in the Dust*, the conflict between the yearning for chivalry and the confrontation with modernity takes shape in a number of World War I stories. In "All the Dead Pilots," the first Bayard's horse has become a machine, a plane, and Jenny's oral narrative (in *Flags* the medium for the hero's survival) has also become a machine, specifically a camera. In "The Leg" and "Crevasse," the conflict focuses on gender: the romantic "valse" between gentleman and lady has become violent sexuality, both male and female.

"The Leg" opens before World War I on a boat on the Thames, from which George speaks, with words and gestures from Spenser, Milton, and Keats, to Everbe Corinthia, whom he sees as a pastoral maiden on shore. Later, George dies in the war; the narrator, Davy, George's friend on that boat, loses his leg and his sanity. Hallucinating, Davy begs George (by now dead) to find his leg and kill it. Meanwhile, Everbe's brother believes Davy has seduced Everbe, betrayed her, driven her mad, and finally caused her death; he comes to attack Davy in the hospital. Although Davy claims that he has been "lying in the hospital talking to George" all the time (*CS*, 841), the brother produces a photograph of Davy inscribed, obscenely, to Everbe Corinthia and showing on Davy's face a "quality vicious and outrageous and unappalled." Acknowledging his acts, Davy nevertheless blames them on his "leg." Quite evidently, the leg to Davy means his phallus; the story suggests that, severed by the war from pre-war civilized control (in a reversal of chivalric assumptions about battle), the phallus inevitably turns next against sexual chivalry, destroying instead of protecting the woman.

In "Crevasse," a party of soldiers, bearing wounded, cross the shell-pocked countryside until they come across the first of many "broad shallow depressions" that strangely bear "no traces of having been made by anything at all' (*CS*, 467). They fall into this natural, unmanmade cave; when the top collapses, the horrific odor of death comes out, and as they struggle to find an exit, they pass dead men standing up in uniform. Finding a hole, they scramble to escape, pushing themselves out into the air and the light. Immediately some pray to the God of the fathers, in thanks at their escape from this tomb. It is no accident, though, that this subterranean crevasse is in "no man's land"; it is woman's territory, here imagined as a tomb-womb that turns against the romance of war, swallowing and destroying uniformed men, sucking live men in instead of birthing them out.

Judging by these stories, liberation from chivalric gender is a high risk process for both sexes. Elsewhere, Faulkner evolved a strategy that reduced the post-chivalric tension between the sexes by yoking them together — in one body. Experimenting with traditional ideas of masculinity in his war stories, Faulkner incorporated into his "new man" aspects of the female. In several instances, he grafts female sexual parts onto (for him) masculine images, such as the plane; in "Death Drag," for example, the pregnant nose "big with engine" joins the phallic potential of the "rigid" propeller "poised and dynamic" (*CS*, 189).[12] Elsewhere, Faulkner makes his hero look girlish but act like a man, so as to add "feminine" characteristics such as innocence, beauty, and sensitivity to the courage of the cavalier. For example, Claude, the British child-soldier in "Turnabout," looks "like a masquerading girl" (*CS*, 475). The American soldiers treat him with a contempt normally reserved for women in war; they say he belongs to a male auxiliary of the WACS, and, when he invites Captain Bogard to go with him on his own war mission, they send along a yellow silk sofa cushion, Japanese parasol, comb, and roll of toilet paper. The turnabout comes when Bogard learns that the boy's apparently frivolous work is far more deadly than his own as a pilot. Bogard acknowledges the boy's virility by sending him a case of Scotch. Claude is the new womanly man; he combines the beauty and innocence of a girl with the courage (and drinking capacity) of a cavalier.[13]

Faulkner also employs typically female psychological experience in his redefined man. As Gail Mortimer shows in *Faulkner's Rhetoric of Loss*,[14] borders and boundaries are normally critical to Faulkner's imagination of individuated identity. Such an obsession is consistent not only with Nancy Chodorow's observations about masculinity, but also with a culture (the South) rigidly defined by boundaries of race, class, and sex. Yet even in the chivalric story from *Flags in the Dust,*

Stuart's men and their horses merge their separate identities into one; on their horses, all the men become "a single centaur" (*FID*, 18). Another World War I story, "Ad Astra," takes as its theme the powers and terrors of borderlessness; in other stories ("Black Music," "Carcassonne") the border between man and animal disappears. Another typically female mode of experience, the non-hierarchical, appears in Faulkner's occasional assertion of brotherhood as an alternative to a patriarchal hierarchy that kills the sons; Captain Bogard in "Turn About," the central character in "Victory," and the sympathetic German in "Ad Astra" despise the "barbarism" of the "hierarchy" implied by the "word *father*" (*CS*, 417).

Perhaps inevitably, Faulkner's imagination played over the meaning not just of masculinity but of traditional female gender as well, creating physically boyish women and women who, like Aunt Jenny in *Flags* and Margaret Powers in *Soldier's Pay*, are heroic in wartime. But that movement released possibilities Faulkner was apparently unwilling to work through. For when he imagines a woman fully outside the patriarchy, the symmetry in his deconstruction of both genders breaks down. Whereas Faulkner's Hisland or Brotherland, with its exclusion of women[15] and its incorporation and expropriation of the feminine, is an ideal to be found in war or on a hunt, Herland is for Faulkner a nightmare. For when women incorporate or expropriate or exclude the male, men lose control; most painfully, they lose authority — sole proprietorship — of the project in hand, namely the deconstruction of gender itself.

Again in *Flags in the Dust* we can find the paradigm: Narcissa Benbow Satoris. When (the second) Bayard Sartoris returns from World War I he marries Narcissa. Yet, in part because she so loves her brother, the womanly Horace, Bayard is a "violation of the very depths of her nature." So when Bayard dies, Narcissa — like a lily after a gale, "untarnished save by the friction of its own petals" (*FID*, 431) — is sad but not sorry he is gone. The female separatism suggested in Faulkner's sexual imagery here (Narcissa implicitly prefers masturbation to heterosexual intercourse) is consistent with her sexual politics, as we will see momentarily; the bitter tone is Faulkner's own. For now Narcissa's project is to reinvent gender by changing the cavalier tradition. She names her son, not Johnny after his father's brother who died a hero in the First World War, but Benbow, after her own family. Narcissa has exercised this authority (as crucial as all naming is in Faulkner) out of specifically female resistance. At first she admires Aunt Jenny Sartoris's "gallantry" and the "uncomplaining steadfastness of those unsung ... women" of the Civil War; she prefers their style to the "fustian and useless glamor of the men that [the women's] was hidden by." Yet now she sees that even Jenny wants to make her "one of [the Sartorises]" and her son "just another rocket to glare for a moment in the sky, then die away" in the cavalier tradition. Thus in authoring her son, in naming him Benbow, Narcissa takes him and hence the future with her one step away from the traditional southern patriarchy; though still a patronymic, Benbow is her own.

But instead of having Narcissa withdraw into sole proprietorship of a fruitful Herland, Faulkner punishes her by placing her into a sterile and false "windless lilac dream, foster-dam of quietude and peace." Women in Faulkner are often connected with vases and jars; Narcissa is here a false Grecian urn, in contrast to Keats' "still unravished bride of quietness ... [and] foster child of silence and slow time."[16] Narcissa is the urn become bell jar, cousin of the crevasse; woman as passive destroyer. When she appears in *Sanctuary*, Faulkner tells us Narcissa is "living a life of serene vegetation like perpetual corn or wheat in a sheltered garden instead of a field."[17] Her serenity now is explicitly called "stupidity" (*S*, 25, 102). And at her autonomous "worst" in "There Was a Queen," Narcissa sits with her son in a stream, suggesting incest; initiates calculated sex for money; and in effect kills Jenny by telling her that she has prostituted herself.

When Ben Wasson, and to some extent Faulkner, revised *Flags* for publication as *Sartoris*, they cut out much of the description of Narcissa's interiority and all of the one entirely autonomous woman, Joan. Along with similar cuts that (Michael Millgate has observed) Faulkner made in *Sanctuary*, such editorial decisions suggest the direction of the next stage of Faulkner's career, insofar as his fictions concerned themselves with gender.[18] After *Flags in the Dust*, sexually or verbally assertive female characters who subvert or stand outside their patriarchal roles will, for Faulkner, be unbalanced. They include Emily Grierson, Elly, Joanna Burden, Temple Drake, Minnie Cooper, and

Mrs. Jim Gant. And the fullest expression of the new womanly man will be the doomed Quentin Compson. The project of reconstructing gender, for Faulkner, is over.

By contrast, it is with precisely the figure of a strong and autonomous woman that Katherine Anne Porter began her writing career. While Faulkner feared that figure, Porter saw her with admiration and hope as a matriarchal alternative to patriarchy. The figure appears in an unsigned sketch in the *Christian Science Monitor* in 1921 that Thomas F. Walsh has identified as Porter's. The sketch, called "Xochimilco," tells of Porter's trip to the Indian village of that name in Mexico.[19] Through an examination of an earlier, still unpublished typescript, Walsh shows that Porter originally began with the image of a powerful goddess, Xochitl, and she titled this version "Children of Xochitl."[20] The predominant religious symbol within the Xochimilco community, Xochitl is the Aztec goddess of the earth and the patroness of women's art (Walsh, 185). "Of all the great women deities," wrote Porter, she has "... the most beneficent attributes." Her nourishing fruitfulness is evident in her connection with maguey, a plant the villagers grow, whose "juice is sucked from the plant" and which, when fermented, is "the color of milk" (Walsh, 186). Finally, as patroness of even the local Christian church, Xochitl has set "her powerful foot" into a "decaying and alien stronghold ... [the patriarchal church] to compete with usurping gods in caring for her strayed family" (Walsh, 184).

Life in Xochimilco is intoxicatingly sensuous and vital. Flowers — their textures, colors, smells — pervade Porter's scene (CSM, 10). The people, too, seem "'a natural and gracious part of the earth they live in such close communion with, entirely removed from contact with the artificial world'" (Walsh, 184). Natural productivity is matched by social; in this Theirland, men, women, and children happily work. Yet community is not identity. As Walsh points out, the people, like the boats they decorate, are as "varied as handwriting." (Walsh, 185). One might add that it is creation from within, rather than conflict with others, that permits individuation; in fact, Porter carefully includes an episode to demonstrate that competition and conflict, though potential, are resolved by a ritual of mutual deference.

Porter's Xochimilco is, in short, a remarkable vision of female power. The goddess Xochitl nurtures a society where rigid borders — between nature and culture, individual and community, indoors and out, even male and female — virtually disappear. The result is not the chaos of lost identity but the rich pleasure of creativity and the ritual resolution of conflict.

Walsh finds in this sketch Porter's "unqualified hope" that the Mexican revolution would "reverse centuries of political and economic oppression" (Walsh, 183). Yet if this is so, he argues, her later stories show increasing pessimism as to its probability. In her downward path to wisdom, Porter finds (I will argue) that because war and revolution are themselves the fullest expressions of patriarchal values, they will infect and destroy those who use them as a means to a new world, including new gendering. In "Flowering Judas,"[21] the chief revolutionary, Braggione, acts like his name. His self-indulgence, his arrogance, and his oppressive sexuality virtually immobilize Laura. Yet as his go-between, she delivers pills to a political prisoner that he uses to kill himself. Xochitl herself reappears in "Hacienda," but she has lost her place of life-giving power in the community. Walsh sees the story as Porter's rewriting of the goddess of life into a goddess of death (Walsh, 183). But the corruption and decay everywhere in "Hacienda" have less to do with a goddess of death than with what the narrator calls "man's confused veneration for, and terror of, the fertility of women and vegetation. . . ." (CS, 165). Veneration in "Hacienda" has given place to terror: a brother kills his sister; Dona Julia looks like an "exotic speaking doll" and her tiny feet "like a Chinese woman's." Patriarchy has won the victory. Xochitl, far from being the goddess of death, has veiled her face; these her later children cannot see her except through their own corrupted vision.

The pattern repeats itself in Porter's World War I story, "Pale Horse, Pale Rider." Miranda works as a newspaper reporter in Denver in 1918. As a member of the public world, she sees the corrupt fictions that sustain both war and traditional gender arrangements. Hucksters use lies and threats to coerce her into buying Liberty Bonds; between the acts of a play, salesmen present a show of war clichés and songs. When Miranda sees her colleague Towney knitting in the women's room, she assumes it is to cheer up some soldier. "Like hell," says Towney. "I'm making this for myself" (CS, 275). Yet when

Towney returns to the newsroom, she is "all open-faced glory and goodness, willing to sacrifice herself for her country," the traditional woman in war (CS, 286). In such a context, public language has lost its connection to truth. As a journalist, Miranda purveys the lies she despises, writing stories "advising other young women to knit and roll bandages and do without sugar and help win the war" (CS, 281).

Miranda privately believes that two fundamental truths, one about war and one about women, have produced the necessity for the patriarchy to fabricate patriotism and femininity. The truth about war is that fathers want to kill their sons. "The tom-cats try to eat the little tom-kittens, you know," she says (CS, 295). The truth about women is that, with the men away, they can be "dangerous." So "rows of young girls," like rows of soldiers, are "given something to keep their little minds out of mischief"; they roll bandages that will never reach a hospital. Yet Miranda keeps her integrity within her private world, where she thinks "To hell with this filthy war" (CS, 273). Although she is falling in love with Adam, a soldier on his way to the war, within that private relationship traditional gender roles are revised. Miranda's work schedule determines their meeting times; when they go out, she takes Adam to a play she is going to review; and when she falls ill, Adam nurses Miranda. As the two move beyond traditional gender roles, so they respond to the war-lies with irony. The war is "simply too good to be true," they say; "I laugh every time I think about it" (CS, 283).

But, ominously, in public they drop the irony. As Miranda writes lies in her work, the two join in the war songs "at the tops of their voices, grinning shamefacedly at each other once or twice" (CS, 294). The power of war, and the risks of such compromises as these, are evident in the effectiveness of the flu, seen as a metaphor for the insidious infiltration of war into civilian life. The flu "wounds" Miranda's body just as her false words wound her integrity. In this way Miranda becomes wholly an agent of the corruption she hates. Ill, she labels her German doctor a "Boche, a spy, a Hun" (CS, 309). Finally, what wounds her kills Adam: she passes the flu to him.

Yet there is one more chance for Miranda, if not for Adam. Close to death herself, she retains a "minute fiercely burning particle of being that knew itself alone, that relied upon nothing beyond itself for its strength" (CS, 310). Trusting that still uncompromised and most private of selves, Miranda has a vision. The particle of being expands into a liminal image. Waves are lapping on sand; grasses are flowing in the wind; people are moving among one another like waves among waves, "alone but not solitary." Earth, air, water, people retain their integrity but experience a continuing process of contact along their "borders." The vision feels warm, peaceful, and rapturous to Miranda. But then she feels a chill: she must return, she feels, to the dead, those still in the actual world. To reenter that world, Miranda must, now self-consciously, reenter a lie. "There is nothing better than to be alive, everyone has agreed on that" (CS, 315), she thinks wryly. Thus "it will not do to betray the conspiracy and tamper with the courage of the living" by exposing the falsity of that convention. And the form of the lie that Miranda chooses is the lie of gender. Sitting in the hospital before the mirror, she writes down her needs: "One lipstick, medium, one ounce flask of Bois d'Hiver perfume, one pair of gray suede gauntlets without straps, two paris gray sheer stockings without clocks"; and she says to herself, this precursor to Plath, "Lazarus, come forth. Not unless you bring me my top hat and stick. ... A jar of cold cream," she continues to write, "a box of apricot powder. ..." (CS, 316). At the end of "Pale Horse, Pale Rider," the new way of loving and (as Walsh calls Miranda's vision) the new version of Xochitl disappear; only the public lies that sustain traditional gender and war survive.

In "The Leaning Tower" (c. 1940), Xochitl does not appear in any form at all, and the fatal connections between war and gender are unequivocal and explicit. Four young men of various nationalities live in a boarding house in Berlin; the widowed landlady's little souvenir tower of Pisa gives the story its name. The American painter Charles inadvertently destroys the (obviously phallic) leaning tower; it collapses at his touch. Thus when the landlady mends the tower in her nostalgia for both her husband and the past, there is a suggestion of the role of women in propping up the patriarchy, for the tower represents not only a man but a masculinized culture. Such a role for women becomes explicit in a scene at a local bar. Charles finds himself attracted to Lutte,[22] a beautiful young German woman. But they dance together awkwardly. Only with the young German Hans von

Gehring does her "manner change completely." Hans wears a dueling scar on his face, emblem of the warrior and the patriarchy. Lutte kisses him "softly and continually and gently on his right cheek, her mouth meek and sweet, her eyes nearly closed. Over Hans' disfigured face came [a] look of full-fed pride, composed self-approval — of arrogance —" (CS, 490). It is Hans who argues against the "worthless feminine" influence and for "pure" masculine "power ... to tell other people what to do, and above all what they may not do" (CS, 486). And it is Hans who insists that there will be another war, which this time Germany will win. Thus two German women, one in her nostalgia and one in her desire, will sustain what Miranda reconstructs, in her despair, at the end of "Pale Horse, Pale Rider": the fiction of traditional gender, which Porter connects to patriarchy and thus to war.

My reading of Faulkner's and Porter's war stories thus tends to confirm the thesis that wars shake up traditional structures, but only temporarily. Deeply disturbed by the wasteland of and after World War I, both Faulkner and Porter connect its horrors with the gender system, which rewards men who exploit hierarchy, conflict, and force, and suppresses the power of the female in both men and women. In some of his stories, Faulkner revises traditional manhood, trying to rescue the best of the chivalric dream by incorporating into it aspects of femaleness such as permeable boundaries, egalitarian community, and sensitivity to feeling. In some of her stories, Porter draws on ancient traditions of female experience and power in an effort to counter the destructiveness of patriarchal society with the creativity she imagines in a matriarchy. Yet both writers fail to sustain this exploration. It is a final and terrible irony that, whereas Faulkner turns away because of his apparent anxiety over the power of the autonomous female, Porter turns away because of her apparent conviction that female autonomy is in fact impossible in a patriarchally gendered world, a world that she feels is doomed not to learn from but to repeat the First World War.

Notes

1. Carol R. Berkin and Clara M. Lovett, eds. *Women, War, and Revolution* (New York: Holmes & Meier, 1980), p. 3.
2. Eric Leed in *No Man's Land: Combat and Identity in the First World War* (Cambridge: Cambridge University Press, 1980) describes the experiences; Sandra Gilbert and Susan Gubar (NEH Summer Seminar, Davis, California, 1981) have made the connection to female experience.
3. Nancy Chodorow, *The Reproduction of Mothering: Psychoanalysis and the Sociology of Gender* (Berkeley: University of California Press, 1979).
4. See, for instance, Barbara J. Steinson, "'The Mother Half of Humanity': American Women in the Peace and Preparedness Movements in World War I," in Berkin and Lovett, pp. 259-276; William J. Breen, "Southern Women in the War: The North Carolina Woman's Committee, 1917-1919," *The North Carolina Historical Review*, LV (July, 1978), and "Black Women and the Great War: Mobilization and Reform in the South," *The Journal of Southern History* XLIV (August, 1978); Ida Clyde Clarke, *American Women and the World War* (New York: D. Appleton, 1918), on the work of the Woman's Committee of the Council of National Defense; Eunice Dessez, *The First Enlisted Women, 1917-1918* (Philadelphia: Dorrance, 1955).
5. William H. Chafe, "The Paradox of Progress," in Jean E. Friedman and William G. Shade, *Our American Sisters: Women in American Life and Thought*, 2nd. ed. (Boston: Allyn and Bacon, 1976), pp. 386-87.
6. Biographical materials taken from: Joan Givner, *Katherine Anne Porter: A Life* (New York: Simon & Schuster, 1982); Joseph Blotner, *Faulkner: A Biography* (New York: Random House, 1974); David Minter, *William Faulkner: His Life and Work* (Baltimore: Johns Hopkins, 1980).
7. Katherine Anne Porter, "Portrait: Old South," in *The Collected Essays and Occasional Writings of Katherine Anne Porter* (New York: Delta, 1973), p. 160.
8. Richard A. Milum, "Continuity and Change: The Horse, the Automobile, and the Airplane in Faulkner's Fiction," in *Faulkner: The Unappeased Imagination, A Collection of Critical Essays*, ed. Glenn O. Carey (Troy, NY: Whitston, 1980), p. 158.
9. William Faulkner, *Flags in the Dust* (New York: Vintage, 1974). Subsequent references will appear in the text in parentheses.
10. The telling of the tale avoids its comic possibilities as it must in order to emphasize the romance and gallantry of risking all for a symbol of culture. Yet Faulkner seems to distance himself from the romantic power of the narration as well, suggesting a bemused or ironic view of its implications, a view that many critics have shared.
11. William Faulkner, *Collected Stories* (New York: Vintage, 1977). Subsequent references will appear in the text in parentheses.
12. This sort of androgyny is apparent elsewhere in Faulkner's fiction. David Minter points to Elmer's tubes of paint "'thick-bodied and female and at the same time phallic: hermaphroditic'" (Minter, 58).
13. Another example of this strategy appears in "Divorce in Naples."
14. Gail Mortimer, *Faulkner's Rhetoric of Loss* (Austin: University of Texas Press, 1984).

15. Actual women don't fit into the Brotherland. When a woman comes between two men, destruction may ensue, as happens in "The Leg," "Divorce in Naples," "Honor," and "All the Dead Pilots." In *Flags* young Bayard thinks of his bedroom as the place where he slept not with either of his wives but with his twin brother John; the wives are latecomers and usurpers, presumably. Near the end of *Flags*, Bayard retreats to the MacCallum household and to Buddy's bed. At this hunting cabin, all the family members are males: they know how to take care of one another.

16. John Keats, "Ode on a Grecian Urn."

17. William Faulkner, *Sanctuary* (New York: Vintage, 1931), p. 103. Subsequent references will appear in the text in parentheses.

18. Michael Millgate, "Faulkner's First Trilogy: *Sartoris, Sanctuary,* and *Requiem for a Nun,*" in *Fifty Years of Yoknapatawpha: Faulkner and Yoknapatawpha, 1979,* ed. Doreen Fowler and Ann J. Abadie (Jackson: University Press of Mississippi, 1980), p. 92.

19. "Xochimilco," *Christian Science Monitor,* May 31, 1921, p. 10. Subsequent references will appear in the text in parentheses.

20. Thomas F. Walsh, "Xochitl: Katherine Anne Porter's Changing Goddess," *American Literature,* LII (May, 1980). Subsequent references will appear in the text in parentheses.

21. Katherine Anne Porter, *The Collected Stories of Katherine Anne Porter* (New York: Plume, 1970), p. 90. Subsequent references will appear in the text in parentheses.

22. In German, *lutte* means duct, pipe, tube, or drain; Porter may be suggesting a female complement to the tower and the dueling sword. Interestingly, the word in French means battle.

The smooth, suave shape of desire: Paradox in Faulkerian imagery of women

GAIL L. MORTIMER

University of Texas, El Paso

CRITICS OF Faulkner have long recognized that his characterizations of women tend to reflect a mythic or primitive imagination. Rather than being fully rounded, his female characters are often stereotypes, incarnations of such qualities as fecundity, serenity, sexual desire, death, or evil. Because we view them only through the (often troubled) consciousness of his male characters and narrators, they attain a degree of reality determined by the quality of the male's awareness that they exist, and they embody characteristics that are essentially projections based on his own needs and anxieties. It is often not possible to determine whether particular perceptions of women should be assumed to be true only for the fictional character or for Faulkner as well. What we can discern is that men in Faulkner's stories who are aware of women are typically troubled by them, and the images in which their perceptions are conveyed to us share important similarities.

Faulkner attributes to some characters a relative indifference to the presence of women. Young boys and old men, for example, experience women as vaguely irritating figures who can, nevertheless, with varying degrees of success, be kept at the periphery of their lives. Faulkner makes it clear that this freedom from a troubling awareness of women is based on a freedom from sexual involvement with them. It is young and middle-aged males who are tormented in his fiction, and

Women's Studies, 1986
Vol. 13, pp. 149-161
0049-7878/86/1302-0149 $18.50/0

when we encounter one who, uncharacteristically, appears not to experience anguish around women, his capacity for aloofness is invariably linked to sexual enervation (V.K. Ratliff, who is celibate; Flem Snopes, who is impotent).

More commonly Faulkner's protagonists are brooding, troubled men whose encounters with women tend to leave them feeling baffled or helpless. Characters like Gavin Stevens, Quentin Compson, Horace Benbow, Harry Wilbourne, and Joe Christmas are consciously preoccupied with racial guilt, the passage of time, death, war, and the deterioration of Southern values, yet they are alike in seeing women as embodying threats somehow basic to their senses of identity. Their own projection onto women of the ambiguities and dilemmas that torment them creates the anguish they experience when with women. These characters are susceptible to degrees of anxiety around women far surpassing what objectively appears justified.

My purpose in this paper is to focus on a particular kind of image that allows Faulkner simultaneously to suggest both the most positive and the most horrifying of masculine responses to the feminine. In his use of bodies of water and of vases and urns as emblems of women, Faulkner is able to combine the attraction and the repulsion felt by his male characters, to suggest both the smooth, alluring surface of the beautiful object and the awareness that a somehow threatening reality lies beneath.

The linkage of women with water is pervasive in myth; Faulkner's particular use of it, however, confirms that woman's sexuality is what makes her threatening. When a woman is not perceived as sexually dangerous, she may be described as a pond (quiet, contained) or other smooth-surfaced body of water. This is true of Narcissa, Horace Benbow's sister, whose very name evokes the image of a pool: "he let himself slip, as into water, into the constant serenity of her affection again" (FD 183).[1] Women who *are* sexually threatening — that is, available and nearby — are seen as bodies of water in turmoil. Notably, in *Flags in the Dust* after Narcissa has been frightened by an encounter with Bayard Sartoris precisely because it awoke sexual feelings, the narrator tells us that she has regained her characteristic peacefulness: "[Bayard] was now no more than the shadow of a hawk's flight mirrored fleetingly by the windless surface of pool, and gone; where, the pool knew and cared not ..." (FD 188-89). In contrast, Caddy, Quentin Compson's sister in *The Sound and the Fury*, is imaged as a river when he begins to believe that incest between them is possible. He becomes obsessed with her and with death. Faulkner writes that Quentin loved death "as a lover loves and deliberately refrains from the waiting willing friendly tender incredible body of his beloved, until he can no longer bear not the refraining but the restraint and so flings, hurls himself, relinquishing, drowning" (TSAF 411). At the last, of course, Quentin does drown himself in a river. In *The Town* Eula Varner terrifies Gavin Stevens by her proximity: "[She was] still not moving: just standing there facing me so that what I smelled was not even just woman but that terrible, that drowning envelopment" (T 95). And Harry Wilbourne looks into Charlotte Rittenmeyer's eyes in *The Wild Palms* and feels himself "to be drowning, volition and will, in the yellow stare" (WP 39). The raging flood in this same novel is a highly comic enactment of man's helplessness in the presence of an overwhelming feminine threat of engulfment.

But if in the notion of woman as body of water Faulkner expresses her apparent fluidity and a consequent anxiety about the eruption of her placid surface into something threatening annihilation, in a complementary image he emphasizes the smooth outer surface itself. With the urn/vase image, he transmutes the anatomy of woman into an emblem of desire and a work of art. As David Minter has argued, the urn is an overdetermined image in which a number of Faulkner's concerns imaginatively converge.[2]

To begin with, it signifies the ideas considered in John Keats's "Ode on a Grecian Urn." The philosophical problem of living within time — the question of whether it is better to be suspended somehow outside of time or to live within time, decaying — so preoccupied Faulkner that he saw his writing as essentially an attempt to transcend time, to leave a "scratch" on "oblivion."[3] He viewed artistic effort as an attempt to deny mutability and decay by creating a trace of something that survives time precisely because it is never fully embodied. Art became an attempt to evoke a world rather than define one, a way of evading the disappointment inherent in living within time by stepping aside from time, suspending existence somehow. We are most familiar with this concern in Faulkner's creation of "frozen moments" wherein his characters appear as if in tableaux, apparently free of time and change.

Keats's "Ode" celebrates just such a suspension of life at what Faulkner believed to be its most perfect — at the height of a moment of desire — by depicting lovers reaching toward one another, never to be disappointed by a reality that must fall short of the desire itself: "yet, do not grieve;/She cannot fade, though thou hast not thy bliss,/For ever wilt thou love, and she be fair!"[4] These few lines became refrains echoed both in Faulkner's writing and in his relationships with women. He repeatedly told Meta Doherty that his greatest concern about their relationship was that it not end "shabbily," in a way unworthy of the beauty they had originally envisioned in it. Once, asked to describe his ideal woman, Faulkner made clear that the evocation of the perfect object existing in the mind is more desirable than its definition or embodiment in some tangible form:

"Well, I couldn't describe her by color of hair, color of eyes, because once she is described, then somehow she vanishes ... the ideal woman which is in every man's mind is evoked by a word or phrase or the shape of her wrist, her hand. . . . And it's best to take the gesture, the shadow of the branch, and let the mind create the tree. So, that's why I couldn't begin to describe my ideal woman ..."[5]

Whether he is speaking of an idea or reality that he hopes to translate into fiction or a woman who seems the idealized vision of his desire, Faulkner refers to "vague shape[s]" of perfection[6] within his imagination of which the actual book or woman can only at best be approximations. Minter discusses this "dilemma of desire," the realization that achieving what you desire inevitably disappoints you because it is never equal to the perfection of the desire itself — the "bright shape" that it took when it was desire alone.[7] Asked whether he ever wished he had written any of his earlier fictions differently, Faulkner responded that there really wasn't time: " 'The best thing is to write another book and do it, because it takes only one book to do it. It's not the sum of a lot of scribbling, it's one perfect book, you see. It's one single *urn* or *shape* that you want to do.' "[8] Keats's urn, then, embodies Faulkner's concerns as an artist and idealist about women by virtue of its existence as an object of beauty surviving time without changing and by perpetuating a moment of ecstasy and desire in the story told by the images on its surface.

Faulkner would at times refer to one of his novels as if it were a vase, characterizing himself as a dignified old man clinging to the vase which symbolized both immortality and desire. Like the speaker of Yeats's "Sailing to Byzantium" — an old man "sick with desire/ And fastened to a dying animal" — he saw his novels as an attempt to take some eternal form, to metamorphose into a beautiful object of art: "such a form as Grecian goldsmiths make/Of hammered gold and gold enamelling/To keep a drowsy Emperor awake[.]"[9] The following passage offers striking evidence of the convergence in Faulkner's imagination of these various images. In an introduction to *The Sound and the Fury* dated August 19, 1933, Faulkner discussed the writing of his favorite among his novels:

"There is a story somewhere about an old Roman who kept at his bedside a Tyrrhenian vase which he loved and the rim of which he wore slowly away with kissing it. I had made myself a vase, but I suppose I knew all the time that I could not live forever inside of it, that perhaps to have it so that I too could lie in bed and look at it would be better; surely so when that day should come when not only the ecstasy of writing would be gone, but the reluctance and the something worth saying too."[10]

Notice his concern with passion and desire ("the ecstasy of writing") on the one hand and the permanence of the created object on the other, with what is necessarily ephemeral and what he hopes will in some sense be immortal.

David Minter connects these images to a final one, that of Caddy, the sister who serves as the imaginative center of the novel. Of the character he saw as his "heart's darling" and "the beautiful one,"[11] Faulkner wrote: " 'I loved her so much I couldn't decide to give her life just for the duration of a short story. She deserved more than that. So my novel was created, almost in spite of myself.' "[12] And elsewhere: " 'I said to myself, Now I can write. Now I can make myself a vase like that which the old Roman kept at his bedside and wore the rim slowly away with kissing it. So I, who never had a sister and was fated to lose my [first] daughter in infancy, set out to make myself a beautiful and tragic little girl.' "[13] Novel, vase, and girl are here thoroughly commingled, symbolically equivalent. Minter writes that Faulkner associated Caddy "with Keats's urn, which he in turn associated with life and with art — with life because it depicted love that was dreamed yet denied, felt yet deferred; and with art because it epitomized form." He sums up the symbolic functions of the urn/vase image:

the vase becomes both Caddy and *The Sound and the Fury*; both 'the beautiful one' for whom he created the novel as a commodious space and the novel in which she found protection and privacy as well as expression. In its basic doubleness the vase is many things: a haven or shelter into which the artist may retreat; a feminine ideal to which he can give his devotion; a work of art that he can leave behind when he is dead; and a burial urn that will contain at least one expression of his self as an artist.[14]

The vase/urn, then, is an image whose meanings go well beyond representing the female body; it involves Faulkner's notions of art, desire, and immortality, as well. Ironically, Faulkner parodies these same meanings by his use of the image in his portrayal of Horace Benbow in *Sanctuary* and *Flags in the Dust*. As critics have long noted, Horace is Prufrockian, inept, and feels passion as a burden. He returns from World War I brooding about death, the war, and the serenity symbolized for him by his sister Narcissa. He has taken up glass blowing, and as if to emphasize the special fragility of the enterprise — the precision needed to stop at the instant of perfection — Faulkner takes care to relate that the many vases he makes are all broken, incomplete, or imperfect in some way. On the boat from Europe, Horace even set his cabin afire blowing one of them. Eventually, after "four mishaps," he "produced one *almost perfect* vase of clear amber, larger, more richly and chastely serene and which he kept always on his night table and called by his sister's name in the intervals of apostrophising both of them impartially in his moments of rhapsody over the realization of the meaning of peace and the unblemished attainment of it, as Thou still unravished bride of quietude" (FD 190-91, emphasis mine).

The idea of keeping a vase on a night table links Horace with Faulkner himself in passages we have looked at. These quotations reveal Faulkner's own variation on the paradigmatic vase in "Ode on a Grecian Urn." He has built into his use of the image evidence of its *inability to remain* the image he desires; it subverts the very messages it might otherwise have conveyed. As an emblem of the object of art, for example, an object whose value for Faulkner is implicit in its suspension in time, its perdurability, Faulkner's vase has an edge worn away with kissing. And he depicts Horace as a maker of glass vases that throughout the novel are stressed as being innately fragile, both imperfect to begin with and breakable.

As an image of woman, too, the vase/urn at times undermines its apparent original meaning. Like his other images that idealize women, the vase suggests a smooth and serene perfection, the approximation, as Minter reminds us, of some "vague shape" of the feminine in Faulkner's mind. In this regard it resembles the marble statues, especially those in the Luxembourg gardens in Paris, that Faulkner found so haunting. But statues differ from vases in one important respect. Their solidity enables them to epitomize the overwhelming lure of the feminine, as it does in a 1925 sketch in which Faulkner juxtaposes a nude female statue and a collapsed male figure.[15] But the vase/urn is an even more fitting image than the statue for conveying Faulkner's concerns because of its interiority; Faulkner is never entirely free of an awareness that a surface overlays an underside of things, felt to be at least potentially corrupt and corrupting. He has Horace confess that he finds life and people " 'all sort of messy: living and seething corruption glossed over for a while by smoothly colored flesh; all foul, until the clean and naked bone' " (FD 337). Faulkner's most troubled protagonists associate women with both physical decay and offensive odor. The striking consequence for his imagery of women is that we frequently find a juxtaposition of what is clean, smooth, pure, and desired with the eruption of something ugly, enveloping, and corrupting. At the center of desire, we find disgust. Joe Christmas has difficulties with women that are part of quite basic dilemmas involving his sense of identity, yet the evolution of his perceptions reveals characteristic Faulknerian modifications of imagery. When Joe is forced to recall something he has long repressed, the fact of menstruation, we are told that he runs away: "In the notseeing and the hardknowing as though in a cave he seemed to see a diminishing row of suavely shaped urns in moonlight, blanched. And not one was perfect. Each one was cracked and from each crack there issued something liquid, deathcolored, and foul. He touched a tree, leaning his propped arms against it, seeing the ranked and moonlit urns. He vomited" (LA 177-78). What is interesting about this passage is not simply Joe's disgust with the feminine, which is obvious enough, but the fact that these "suavely shaped urns" draw him near and then reveal themselves to be imperfect. They fail to keep the promise of perfection implied by their shape, fail to have been equal to the desire.

In *Flags in the Dust* and *Sanctuary* Faulkner juxtaposes the ideas of what is pure and what is corrupting in image patterns contrasting Narcissa Benbow and Belle Mitchell. Narcissa is associated in her brother's mind with serenity and images of smooth surfaces; Belle, sexually involved with Horace, is associated with turmoil and danger, darkness and odors. Horace refers to the vase and his sister alike as "still unravished bride[s]" and thinks of the vase he names for her as "chastely serene" (FD 190): "his sister beyond the lamp from him filled the room with that constant untroubling serenity of hers in which his spirit drowsed like a swimmer on a tideless summer sea" (FD 189). Passages about Belle are quite different. They suggest that even when she is out of sight, her sexuality pervades the air Horace breathes: "beyond the black and motionless trees Belle's sultry imminence was like a presence, like the odor of death" (FD 228); "somewhere, everywhere, behind and before and about them pervading, the dark warm cave of Belle's rich discontent and the tiger-reek of it" (FD 223).

More characteristic than this complete separation of the two kinds of imagery is Faulkner's placing of them within a single image — apparently benign surface and destructive reality beneath. In *Sanctuary* Horace is entangled in the expectations and needs of three women; he envisions them all together "and himself like one of those furious and aimless bugs that dart with sporadic and unbelievable speed upon the surface of the stagnant water as though in furious escape from the very substance that spawned them" (S 254). Many elements of male anxiety in the presence of the female are evident here: women as water, the source of life, somehow corrupt; male as trying to escape, anxious and furious, drawn toward the surface of something that will trap him. What is said of Horace as he first feels the lure of sexuality seems true of several of Faulkner's protagonists and perhaps of Faulkner himself: "the world was opening out before him ... filled with shadowy shapes of dread and of delight not to be denied" (FD 223-24).

In her account of her long-time love affair with Faulkner, Meta Carpenter Wilde (née Doherty) suggests that he indeed felt profound ambivalence toward women, that they represented both "shapes of dread and of delight." His letters and poems to her are alternately very carnal and deeply romantic; he tended to refer to the physical and the ideal in startling combinations. Wilde expresses her bewilderment at one manifestation of this duality in Faulkner's imagination. He tended, as he apparently did with others, to treat her as if she were still a young girl on the *verge* of sexuality. The difference in their ages, she writes, had for him

strangely widened. Although he made love to me as a man to a woman, there were times when he saw me as being far younger than I was. A girl-child. With one flourish of his mental blue pencil, he would edit out all the facts of my life since Memphis. . . . I don't remember making an effort to play my assigned part at these times, for, if anything, I was confounded by his need to turn me into a sweet, tremulous girl.[16]

David Minter has analyzed this trait, quite accurately, I believe, as essentially Faulkner's attempt to turn Meta back into "an acceptably pure shape — that of a young girl."[17] He concludes, "The move of a young girl through puberty to sexuality seemed to [Faulkner] almost to epitomise the Fall."[18] Although Faulkner associated sexuality with passion and idealism, he also experienced in it a sense of sin and a fall into physicality. After a long separation, the lovers were reconciled, and Wilde writes: "I had almost forgotten until our renewed intimacy Faulkner's curious physical tidiness when he was with me. He was obsessed with keeping from me the grossness of his physical self, running the water in the bathroom to cover the evidence of his animality, bathing each time we made love."[19]

Telling evidence of a split in Faulkner's imagination between the carnal and the idealized is found in a letter he wrote to Wilde in 1939, when she was married to someone else. Here the vase image, which earlier he had extolled as symbolizing the beauty of art and of woman, is itself transmuted. She writes, "He protested that he didn't see me enough and that it was bad, physically, to live as he was now. He knew that he should find a girl ('a physical spittoon,' he phrased it), but although he had tried, he was unable to."[20] And this, to a former lover!

Faulkner's stories reveal another variation on this dualistic imagery. Writing of highly sexual women, he tended to use images which, apart from their overt content, imply the threat of bursting; an apparently placid surface threatens to (or actually does) collapse or break, revealing some unnameable, terrifying substratum. Eula Varner in *The Hamlet*, even in her early teens, is described in terms of her burgeoning thighs and breasts and the narrator's inability to imagine how her clothes can contain them: "[She emanated] that outrageous quality of being, existing, actually on the outside of the garments she wore . . ."(H 101). She and other women seen as sexually intimidating also generate images of grape arbors (cf. the names Dewey Dell and Lena Grove): "her entire appearance suggested some symbology out of the old Dionysic times — honey in sunlight and bursting grapes, the writhen bleeding of the crushed fecundated vine beneath the hard rapacious trampling goat-hoof" (H 95). Horace Benbow is preoccupied with Belle's daughter, Little Belle, as she begins to spend time with boys: "Each spring he watched the reaffirmation of the old ferment, the green-snared promise of unease. . . . Little Belle's voice would seem to be the murmur of the wild and waxing grape itself. . . . the delicate and urgent mammalian rifeness of that curious small flesh" (S 14). Again, we find Horace "thinking of the grape arbor . . . of that curious small flesh in which was vatted delicately a seething sympathy of the blossoming grape" (S 145).

Further corroboration that such images convey anxiety at the prospect of surfaces collapsing is a reference Faulkner makes to *Madame Bovary*. Twice in *Sanctuary* he has Horace recall the scene in which black liquid spills out of the dead woman's mouth onto her white burial gown. In one version Horace dreams about his mother; she is talking to him, and he tries to look away: "But it was too late. He saw her mouth open; a thick, black liquid welled in a bursting bubble that splayed out upon her fading chin . . . and he was thinking He [Popeye] smells black. He smells like that black stuff that ran out of Bovary's mouth when they raised her head" (S 60). Notice that Faulkner has elaborated on this awful moment in *Madame Bovary* by adding precisely the detail that the liquid first forms a bubble which then bursts. He adds the momentary coherence of the bubble to his recollection of the novel; no mention of a bubble appears in Flaubert's narrative.

With such imagery in mind, we find fuller significance in Faulkner's descriptions of Horace's glass vases. Horace would name each new vase and bring it to his sister: "And as he finished them and before they were scarce cooled, he must bring them across the lawn to where she sat . . . in his stained dishevelled clothes and his sooty hands in which the vase lay *demure and fragile as a bubble*" (FD 228, emphasis mine). The importance to Faulkner of the idea of fragility seems unmistakable; as I have suggested, his imagined vases differ from Keats's urn in their inherent tenuousness. What the urn/vase (and the grape, bubble, and body of water) connotes, it implicitly also subverts. Evoking the shape of a woman, these images convey the idea of a surface/shape attracting a man and then entrapping or enveloping him. The reality of proximity to a woman threatens something loathsome. It is little wonder that a powerful sense of blurred personal boundaries accompanies the anxiety Faulkner's troubled protagonists experience when they are too close to women: smells and sounds they cannot escape (consider the interiority of these senses); feelings of drowning; panic; vomiting; collapse.

What these image patterns suggest is that a particular kind of Faulknerian character experiences women in archaic ways. Faulkner projects onto his characters a decidedly limited number of attitudes toward — and experiences of — women. To a few of them, women are fairly innocuous, if not benign. To others, especially the artist figures he often created early in his career, they represent an ideal probably impossible to attain. But to still others, women, as both "shapes of dread and of delight," convey an irrefutable knowledge of the physical. Precisely those characters obsessed with the passage of time, with mortality and death, find in women too immediate an experience of the physical, unavoidable reminders of personal deterioration, decay, and death. Like the earliest Church Fathers, these characters associate women with materiality, with sin and damnation, with the presence of evil in the world. Horace philosophizes about women and evil: "'Not that there is evil in the world; evil belongs in the world: it is the mortar in which the bricks are set. It's that [women] can be so impervious to the mire which they reveal and teach us to abhor; can wallow without tarnishment in the very stuff in the comparison with which their bright, tragic, fleeting magic lies'" (S 282). Woman's is "the smooth and superior shape" (LA 173) embodying this "bright, tragic, fleeting magic" so alluring to males. Yet, like Temple Drake in *Sanctuary*, she is irremediably linked to evil, to death.

The concerns symbolized by the images discussed above are those of the Romantic poet. Like his "Ode on a Grecian Urn," John Keats's "Ode on Melancholy" brings together images and meanings we have found potent for Faulkner: the convergence of beauty and sadness, mortality and vulnerability felt most poignantly at the moment of ecstasy, "aching Pleasure," "Beauty that must die." Both project onto woman their "wakeful anguish of the soul."

She [Melancholy] dwells with Beauty — Beauty that must die;
And Joy, whose hand is ever at his lips
Bidding adieu; and aching Pleasure nigh,
Turning to Poison while the bee-mouth sips:
Ay, in the very temple of delight
Veil'd Melancholy has her sovran shrine,
Though seen of none save him whose strenuous tongue
Can burst Joy's grape against his palate fine;
His soul shall taste the sadness of her might,
And be among her cloudy trophies hung.[21]

Notes

1. References to Faulkner's novels appear in parentheses in the text with the relevant page numbers. The following abbreviations are used (original publication dates are listed before the data on the edition used): FD = *Flags in the Dust* (1973; New York: Random House, Vintage, 1974); H = *The Hamlet*, 3rd ed. (1964; New York: Random House, Vintage, 1972); LA = *Light in August* (1932; New York: Random House, Vintage, 1972); S = *Sanctuary: The Original Text*, ed. Noel Polk (New York: Random House, 1981); TSAF = *The Sound and the Fury* (1929; New York: Random House, Vintage, 1954); T = *The Town* (1957; New York: Random House, Vintage, 1961); WP = *The Wild Palms* (1939; New York: Random House, Vintage, 1964).
2. David Minter, *William Faulkner: His Life and Work* (Baltimore, Md: Johns Hopkins, 1980), esp. pp. 99-103.
3. James B. Meriwether and Michael Millgate, eds., *Lion in the Garden: Interviews with William Faulkner 1926-1962* (New York: Random House, 1968), pp. 227 and 253; see also Minter, p. 240.

4. H.W. Garrod, ed., *Keats: Poetical Works* (Oxford, England: Oxford University Press, 1970), pp. 209-10.
5. *Lion in the Garden*, pp. 127-28.
6. In "Elmer," William Faulkner Collections, Alderman Library, University of Virginia, Charlottesville; quoted in Minter, pp. 56-58.
7. Minter, p. 64.
8. Frederick L. Gwynn and Joseph L. Blotner, eds., *Faulkner in the University: Class Conferences at the University of Virginia 1957-58* (Charlottesville: The University of Virginia Press, 1959), p. 65, emphasis mine.
9. *The Collected Poems of W.B. Yeats* (New York: The Macmillan Company, 1956), pp. 191-92.
10. Jill Faulkner Summers Private Archive; quoted in Joseph Blotner, *Faulkner: A Biography* (New York: Random House, 1974), pp. 811-12.
11. *Faulkner in the University*, p. 6.
12. From Maurice Coindreau's introduction to his French translation of *The Sound and the Fury*; repr. in translation in *The Mississippi Quarterly*, 19 (Summer 1966), 109.
13. In James B. Meriwether, "Faulkner: Lost and Found," *The New York Times Book Review*, Nov. 5, 1972, p. 7.
14. Minter, pp. 56 and 102, respectively.
15. *The Scream*, May 1925, Vol. 1, No. 5, p. 14; repr. in *William Faulkner: Early Prose and Poetry*, comp. Carvel Collins (London: Jonathan Cape, 1963), pp. 105 and 133. This sketch portrays a collapsed man, his clothing partially torn off, in front of a statue of a nude woman.
16. Meta Carpenter Wilde and Orin Borsten, *A Loving Gentleman: The Love Story of William Faulkner and Meta Carpenter* (New York: Simon and Schuster, 1976), p. 77.
17. Minter, p. 163.
18. Minter, p. 109. Blotner tells us that as he realized his daughter Jill was growing up, Faulkner once said sadly: "'It's over very soon. This is the end of it. She'll grow into a woman.'" *Faulkner*, p. 1169.
19. Wilde and Borsten, p. 279.
20. Wilde and Borsten, p. 244.
21. *Keats: Poetical Works*, pp. 219-20.

Pheoby's hungry listening

ALICE REICH

Regis College, Denver

I LIKE TO THINK that Zora Neale Hurston would be happy to be an anthropologist today, that she would come to our feminist studies with the same energy and skepticism that she brought to her studies of folklore, that she would feel affirmed by what we are doing and prod us to go beyond that. I wondered particularly, as I read *Their Eyes Were Watching God,* what she would think of the work of Nancy Chodorow, Carol Gilligan (and many others now) who point the way to a model of female development that is very different from male development, to a female myth that does not look so much like the journey of Odysseus as the growth patterns of a tree or the phases of the moon. And I hope she would indulge me as I attempt to read the story of her Janie as a particularly female myth, for I do this with respect not only for all I can see in Janie, but also for all I cannot see.[1]

In a book rich with imagery and black oral tradition, Zora Neale Hurston tells us of a woman's journey that gives the lie to Freud's assertion that "the difficult development which leads to femininity seems to exhaust all the possibilities of the individual."[2] On the contrary, Janie finds her self and her voice by working through and finally transcending the limiting images of woman as servant, as wife, as romantic lover. She finds herself through relationship with others and she finds her voice, finally, through "Pheoby's hungry listening." (p. 23)

Janie's self is a given, a jewel inside her that is there from the beginning, as it is in all people:

Women's Studies, 1986
Vol. 13, pp. 163-169
0049-7878/86/1302-0163 $18.50/0

When God had made The Man, he made him out of stuff that sung all the time and glittered all over. Then after that some angels got jealous and chopped him into millions of pieces, but still he glittered and hummed. So they beat him down to nothing but sparks but each little spark had a shine and a song. So they covered each one over with mud. (pp. 138-139)

Janie's journey is her struggle against the forces that cover her jewel with mud and silence her singing, and the forces ranged against her are the obstacles encountered both by black people in their historical struggle and by women in our individual struggle. For a time, these forces silence her and subvert her sensuality into subordination.

Janie first awakens to her sensuality early in the novel in an orgasmic communion with nature as she lies dreaming beneath a pear tree (p. 24); and ever after she "saw her life like a great tree in leaf" (p. 20). But at this first shine of her jewel, Janie's grandmother, seeing the danger of a bad marriage, or a pregnancy without marriage, transfers Janie to her first husband, Logan Killicks, a steady, economically independent man. Thus, *Their Eyes Were Watching God* is a chronicle of sanctioned attempts to silence Janie's voice and her sense of herself. Janie is first silenced as black women in slavery were silenced. She is redefined not as a pear tree, but as "branches without roots"; Janie's grandmother "wanted to preach a great sermon about colored women sittin' on high, but they wasn't no pulpit for me" (pp. 31-32). Janie is also silenced in the way that, as Carol Gilligan observes, adolescent females are characteristically silenced:

a silencing enforced by the wish not to hurt others but also by the fear that, in speaking, her voice will not be heard. . . . [There is a] mysterious disappearance of the female self in adolescence. . . . [It becomes] an underground world kept secret because it is branded by others as selfish and wrong.[3]

Janie tries to tell her grandmother that "the vision of Logan Killicks was desecrating the pear tree, but Janie didn't know how to tell Nanny that" (p. 28).

So Janie marries not a man but sixty acres and protection; even so she hopes for "things sweet wid mah marriage lak when you sit under a pear tree and think" (p. 43). She waits "a bloom time, and a green time and an orange time," but discovers "that marriage did not make love. Janie's first dream [is] dead, so she [becomes] a woman" (pp. 43-44), a woman in a loveless marriage, physically repelled by her husband. Little better than a farm animal, she is fed and not mistreated so long as she works.

Janie and Killicks do not speak much to one another at all. She talks to falling seeds, and she looks up the road. Down the road comes Joe Starks, not "pollen and blooming trees" but "far horizon . . . change and chance" (p. 50). She leaves Logan Killicks and goes off with Joe, hoping to revive her first feelings of herself:

From now on until death she was going to have flower dust and springtime sprinkled over everything. A bee for her bloom. Her old thoughts were going to come in handy now, but new words would have to be made and said to fit them. (pp. 54-55)

In his material success and political power as storeowner and mayor of the all-black community of Eatonville, Joe Starks represents another real step up from slavery. However, in his bourgeois life, a man must have (own) a wife to display his success. Janie is there to receive material things ("Joe didn't make many speeches with rhymes to her, but he bought her the best things" [p. 56]); she is an object in his store (p. 87). With Killicks, Janie had had no place ("You ain't got no particular place. It's wherever Ah need yuh" [p. 52]); with Joe Starks, "she's uh woman and her place is in de home" (p. 69).

What Janie likes best about Eatonville are the gatherings around words, the speech-making, sermonizing, story-telling, singing, and "woofing," but Joe forbids her participation. His is the big voice in his community and it defines and silences Janie; "mah wife don't know nothin' 'bout no speech-makin'" (p. 69). And once again Janie's pear tree withers without her voice: ("It must have been the way Joe spoke without giving her a chance to say anything one way or another that took the bloom off of things." [p. 70]) Janie comes to know the dual consciousness of the wife, the woman who has feelings but no voice to express them. "She didn't change her mind but she agreed with her mouth." (p. 99) And, "gradually, she pressed her teeth together and learned to hush," losing her "petal-openness" (p. 111):

She had no more blossomy openings dusting pollen over her man, neither any glisten-ing young fruit where the petals used to be. . . . She had an inside and an outside now and suddenly she knew how not to mix them. (pp. 112-113)

Janie intends to stay in her marriage in spite of its costs to her, in spite of her knowledge that it does not have anything other than a public meaning anymore. She says, "Maybe he ain't nothin' . . . but he is something in my mouth. He's got to be else Ah ain't got nothin' to live for. Ah'll lie and say he is" (p. 118). Because her life and her outside voice are a lie, the injustice of her situation finally drives her to use her own true voice: Joe teases her about her age and looks and she returns the barb in front of other men. When she stops reflecting back to him his own magnified image, Joe is shattered: "Joe Starks didn't know the words for all this, but he knew the feeling" (p. 124). And he sickens and dies, believing that Janie has poisoned him. Though she comes to understand some of the difficulties of his life, she never sees how they could have been resolved: "She thought back and forth about what happened in the making of a voice out of a man" (p. 134). And at the same time she remembers that there is a free girl self still in her, and this self rollicks "with the springtime across the world" while she sends her face to Joe's funeral (p. 137).

There remains one major adventure that Janie has not had, one relationship to work through before she can claim her self. "She was saving up her feelings for some man she had never seen" (p. 112). Janie now has the "luxury" of romantic love. She has never found a man who might be to her as "a bee to a blossom — a pear tree blossom in the spring" (p. 161). She knows that she is not interested in any of the Eatonville men who come to court the well-to-do widow and she enjoys her freedom, even her loneliness. But in the store "it always seemed to her that she was still clerking for Joe and that soon he would come in and find something wrong that she had done" (p. 141). And Janie cannot free herself from that. She needs a man, but not just any man. She needs a man who will not merely repeat what her first two husbands have done, to use her solely for their own ends; she needs a man who will free her by loving the hidden parts of her self. And along comes Tea Cake, who wants her to play, to sing, to tell stories. But most of all, along comes Tea Cake who "looked like the love thoughts of women. . . . Crushing aromatic herbs with every step he took. Spices hung about him. He was a glance from God" (p. 161). Once again in Janie's life "new thoughts had tuh be thought and new words said," but this time Janie is saying them, for Tea Cake has taught her "de maiden language all over" (p. 173).

Janie leaves Eatonville with Tea Cake, explaining to her friend Pheoby that it may not make "business" sense, but it is love; that she has lived the life her Grandmother wanted for her, and it is now time to live her own:

[Grandmother] was borned in slavery time when folks, dat is black folks, didn't sit down any time dey felt lak it. So sittin' on porches lak de white madam looked lak uh mighty fine thing tuh her. Dat's whut she wanted for me — don't keer what it cost. Git up on uh high chair and sit dere. She didn't have time tuh think whut tuh do after you got up on de stool uh do nothin'. De object wuz tuh git dere. So Ah got up on de high stool lak she told me, but Pheoby, Ah done nearly languished tuh death up dere. Ah felt like de world wuz crying' extry and Ah ain' read de common news yet." (p. 172)

Tea Cake is a route to herself for Janie. He embodies all that she had to silence to survive as Joe Starks' wife; dreaming and living his dreams, the antithesis of a materialist, he is life and joy; Janie loves him. But Janie's love for Tea Cake poses the contradiction that all women in patriarchal society find in heterosexual love. Her grandmother has warned her "Dat's de very prong all us black women gits hung on. Dis love!" (p. 41). But for Janie it is only with this "self-crushing love" that "her soul crawled out from its hiding place" (p. 192).

Tea Cake takes Janie to the Everglades where she finds a freedom she has never known, a classless society based on manual labor and good times. Janie and Tea Cake's love is blissful. She works with him, not for him; she joins in the story-telling and is no longer silent; her feelings and her words, her self and her man are all unified. But Janie herself never sees the limitations in the way he defines her, though they are there for the reader to see. She is so in love with him that her place is wherever he wants it to be (p. 219), that she is able to let him slap "her around a bit to show he was boss" (p. 218), that she waits for him at home or goes with him to work, as he wishes. With Tea Cake, Janie has found the love she has dreamed of (and its contradictions, of which she remains unaware). With Tea Cake, Janie finds a way to herself, but it is not until she no longer has Tea Cake that Janies finds her self.

Into the unity of "the muck" comes the chaos of a hurricane, confounding the categories of human and animal, life and death, love and hate. As Janie and Tea Cake are trying to escape, he is bitten by a rabid dog, a dog who "wuzn't nothin' all over but pure hate. Wonder where he come from?" (p. 247) The mad dog of hate transforms Tea Cake and in his madness he attacks Janie, who kills him in self defense. She loved him, but she is not at all paralyzed by his loss. She goes to her trial where she tells her story and "make[s] them see" (p. 278). She arranges his funeral where, in contrast to her experience at Joe's funeral, "She was too busy feeling grief to dress like grief" (p. 281). And she returns to Eatonville where, in her story to Pheoby, which constitutes the bulk of the book's narrative, her life, her thoughts, her feelings, and her words are finally unified.

Janie had been angry at her grandmother for having "taken the biggest thing God ever made, the horizon ... and pinched it in to such a little bit of a thing that she could tie it about her granddaughter's neck tight enough to choke her" (p. 138). Through following her own dreams however, she has been "tuh de horizon and back" (p. 284). And she ends with that horizon over her shoulder "like a great fishnet. ... So much of life in its meshes! She called in her soul to come and see" (p. 286). Janie finds herself through other people and is, in this, very female. Her living through first her grandmother's dream for her, then the dream of a materialistic society, and finally her own dream of love is not a sign of weakness, but of a female way of being in the world that emphasizes attachment and relationship rather than separation and achievement.

Notes

1. Having read this book in the company of women (those published here), I cannot claim any of these ideas as my own. It is equally difficult to acknowledge any particular sources, but Pam Annas, Anne Jones and I collaborated on a paper that had at least the germs of most of these thoughts. I hear the voices of two of my students and friends, Willow Simmons and Ken Pimple, when I think about female myth. But the ideas are all coming through me now, and I voice them in

their imperfection. All references to *Their Eyes Were Watching God* are to the University of Illinois Press edition.
2.   Quoted in Phyllis Chesler, *Women and Madness*. New York: Avon Books, 1973, p. 93.
3.   Carol Gilligan, *In a Different Voice: Psychological Theory and Women's Development*. Cambridge, Mass: Harvard University Press, 1982, p. 51.

Notes about contributors

PAMELA J. ANNAS teaches English at the University of Massachusetts, Boston; she has written on Sylvia Plath and Charlotte Perkins Gilman, among other figures.

JUDITH PUCHNER BREEN teaches English at San Francisco State University and is preparing a study of twentieth-century women novelists and their nineteenth-century precursors.

SANDRA M. GILBERT AND SUSAN GUBAR, co-authors of *The Madwoman in the Attic: The Woman Writer and the Nineteenth-Century Literary Imagination* and co-editors of the *Norton Anthology of Literature by Women*, are working "No Man's Land: The Place of the Woman Writer in the Twentieth Century." Sandra Gilbert teaches English at Princeton University; Susan Gubar is a member of the English Department at Indiana University, Bloomington.

ANNE GOODWYN JONES's book, *Tomorrow is Another Day: The Woman Writer in the South, 1859-1936,* won the Jules F. Landry Prize from Louisiana State University Press in 1981; she teaches at the University of Florida, serves on the advisory board of *PMLA*, and is now at work on a feminist reading of the literature of the Southern Renaissance.

BARBARA LOOTENS is in the English Department at Purdue University North Central, Westiville, Indiana, where she has just developed a course on motherhood in American fiction.

Women's Studies, 1986
Vol. 13, pp. 171-173
0049-7878/86/1302-0171 $18.50/0

© Gordon and Breach Science Publishers, Inc., 1986
Printed in Great Britain

LINDA MIZEJEWSKI, who teaches English at Wheeling College in West Virginia, has published numerous articles on women and literature in such journals as *JEGP, College English* and *Georgia Review*, as well as poems in many periodicals; this year she was awarded a James Still Fellowship by the University of Kentucky.

GAIL L. MORTIMER, who teaches at the University of Texas, El Paso, is the author of *Faulkner's Rhetoric of Loss*, University of Texas Press.

CARYN MUSIL is Associate Professor of English at La Salle College and the Director of the National Women's Studies Association; she is currently working on a book about Mrs Humphrey Ward.

JEAN PICKERING is Professor and Chair of English at California State University, Fresno; an active member of the Doris Lessing Society, she has published on Lessing in *Modern Fiction Studies* and is at present writing a long essay on the British short story from World War II to the present.

ALICE REICH teaches Anthropology, Sociology and Women's Studies at Regis College in Denver and makes frequent appearances at other campuses to give a slide-lecture on goddesses; her current research is in feminist spirituality.

CAROLE STONE has published two chapbooks of poetry, *Legacy* and *A Sentimental Education*, as well as articles on "Mothers and Daughters" and "Fathers and Daughters"; she teaches English at Montclair State College in New Jersey.

EILEEN WIZNITZER teaches writing and studies psychology in Boston; she is at work on a book about *The Waste Land's* portraits of women.

JEAN WYATT, an Associate Professor of English and Comparative Literature at Occidental College, has had articles on Virginia Woolf in several journals, including *PMLA* and *Mosaic*; at present, she is working on a book about female fantasy construction.

MELODY M. ZAJDEL is an Associate Professor of English at Montana State University; she has published essays about H.D. and Caresse Crosby and is currently co-ordinator of the Northwest Women's Studies Association.